# Finding Peace in God

# Finding Peace in God

## CHARLES SPURGEON

**W** *Whitaker House*

All Scripture quotations are taken from the *King James Version* (KJV) of the Bible.

## FINDING PEACE IN GOD

ISBN: 0-88368-502-7
Printed in the United States of America
Copyright © 1997 by Whitaker House

Whitaker House
30 Hunt Valley Circle
New Kensington, PA 15068

1 2 3 4 5 6 7 8 9 10 11 12 13 / 06 05 04 03 02 01 00 99 98 97

# Contents

**Chapter 1**

## Comfort to Those Who Seek God

*"I have not spoken in secret, in a dark place of the
earth: I said not unto the seed of Jacob, Seek ye
me in vain."*
—Isaiah 45:19

What God has said in His Word is inexpressibly full of comfort and delight. Yet, we may also gain much solace by considering what He has not said, for this will give us a great amount of comfort as well. It was one of these *"said not*[s]*"* that preserved the kingdom of Israel in the days of Jeroboam, the son of Joash, for *"the LORD said not that he would blot out the name of Israel from under heaven"* (2 Kings 14:27).

In the above verse from Isaiah, we have an assurance that God will answer prayer, because He has not said to the seed of Israel, *"Seek ye me in vain."* You may be thinking some bitter thoughts against yourself. However, I want you to remember that, no matter what your doubts and fears say, if God has not cut you off from mercy there is no room for despair. Even the voice of your conscience is of little weight if it is not seconded by the voice of God.

Tremble at what God has said! But do not allow your own fears and suspicions to overwhelm you with despondency and sinful despair.

Many timid people have been distressed by the suspicion that there may be something in God's decree that shuts them out from all hope, some secret, written in the great roll of destiny, which renders it certain that if they did pray and seek the Lord, He would not be found by them. Our text is a complete refutation of that troublesome fear. *"I have not spoken in secret, in a dark place of the earth: I said not,* [even in the secret of My unsearchable decree] *Seek ye me in vain."* God has told us everything we need to know, because, while the decrees are *"spoken in secret"* and hidden as *"in a dark place of the earth,"* it is absolutely certain that the Lord has said nothing in any of them or anywhere else that can be interpreted to mean, *"Seek ye me in vain."*

Oh, no, the truth that God has so clearly revealed, that He will hear the prayer of those who call upon Him, cannot be contradicted by anything that God may have spoken elsewhere. He has so firmly, so truthfully, so righteously spoken that there can be no equivocation. He does not, like the Sibyls, speak mysteriously with a double tongue, or, like the Delphic oracle, reveal His mind in unintelligible words, but He speaks plainly and positively, *"Ask, and ye shall receive"* (John 16:24). Oh, that all of you would accept this sure truth: that prayer must and will be heard, and that never, even in the secrets of eternity, never, even in the council chamber of the covenant, has the Lord said to any living soul, *"Seek ye me in vain."*

I want to discuss the fact that those who seek God through Jesus Christ in God's own appointed way cannot, by any possibility, seek Him in vain. Earnest, penitent, prayerful hearts, though they may be delayed for a time, can never be sent away with a final denial. *"Whosoever shall call upon the name of the Lord shall be saved"* (Rom. 10:13). *"Every one that asketh receiveth; and he that seeketh findeth; and to him that knocketh it shall be opened"* (Matt. 7:8). I will prove this, first, by the negative statement, as our text has it: *"I said not: seek ye me in vain,"* and then, briefly, by the positive perspective. Through this study, may God give us His Holy Spirit, so that comfort may be given to many troubled hearts.

## POSITIVE TRUTH FROM A NEGATIVE STATEMENT

It is not possible that a man should sincerely seek for mercy and eternal life in God's own appointed way and not find it. It is not possible that a man should earnestly pray to God from his heart, and yet a gracious answer be finally refused. And there are several reasons for that.

### God Does Not Command Us to Pray in Vain

We will suppose the following case: if sincere prayer could be fruitless, then the question arises, Why, then, are men exhorted to pray at all? If prayer is not heard, if supplication may possibly end in a failure, why does God so constantly, so earnestly, so strenuously compel and command men to call upon Him?

Would it not be a heartless cruelty on my part if I saw a poor farmer who could not pay his way and I exhorted him to plow over a rock and scatter the little seed he had upon soil where I knew it could never grow? Or if a king imposed upon his poor subject a law that the subject should plow the seashore and cultivate it and exercise all the skills of farming upon it, when the king was perfectly aware that not a single grain could ever bless the farmer's toil? What would you think of any man who would advise a thirsty wretch to pump an empty well? Suppose some sovereign would command his subject, seeing he is ready to die of thirst, to let the bucket down where there is no water and to continue to do it without ceasing—to be always letting down the bucket, and always winding it up—with the absolute certainty that no good can come of it!

And do you think that God, who commands men to pray and not to faint, would direct them do it, if no harvest could be reaped from it? Does He not tell them to continue in prayer, to pray without ceasing, to watch unto prayer, to arise in the night watches and cry to Him? After all this, has He then decided that He will be deaf to their entreaties and despise their cries?

Would it not be a piece of heartless tyranny if a king should visit a man in his condemned cell and encourage the prisoner to petition his favor, more than that, command him to do it when he had no intention of giving it? What if this sovereign said to him, "If I do not send you an answer at once, send another petition and another; send to me seven times. Yes, continue to do it, and never cease as long as you live. Be persistent, and you will prevail." And what if the king should tell the man the story of the persistent widow, should describe to him the case of the man who, by perseverance, obtained the three loaves for his weary friend? What if he said to the condemned man, "In the same way, if you ask, you will receive," and yet all the while never intended to pardon the man? What if he had determined in his heart that the man's death warrant should be signed and sealed, and that on the execution morning he should be launched into eternity?

I ask you whether this is consistent with royal generosity, whether this is fit conduct for a gracious monarch. And can you for a moment suppose that God would tell you, as He does each one of us, to seek His face—would He invite you to come to Him through Jesus Christ—and yet, secretly in His heart, intend never to be gracious at the voice of your cry?

### God Is Not Deaf to Our Prayers

If prayer could be offered continuously, and God could be sought earnestly, but no mercy could be found, then he who prays would be worse off than he who does not pray. Supplication would be an ingenious invention for increasing the sufferings of mankind. For a man who does not pray has less sorrow than a man who does pray, if God does not answer prayer.

The man who prays is made to hunger: will he hunger and not eat? Is it not, then, better never to hunger? How then can it be said, *"Blessed are they which do hunger and thirst after righteousness"* (Matt. 5:6)? The man who prays, thirsts. *"As the hart panteth after the water brooks"* (Ps. 42:1), so he

11

pants after his God. But if God will never give him the living water to drink, is not a thirsty soul much more wretched than one who never learned to thirst at all?

He who has been taught to pray has great desires and needs. His heart is an aching void that the world can never fill. But he who never prays has no longings for God. He who never makes any supplication feels no ungratified desires for eternal things. If, then, a man may have these vehement longings, but God will never grant them, then assuredly the man who prays is in a worse position than he who does not pray. How can this be? Has God so constituted the world that virtue will entail misery and that vice will engender happiness? Can it be, while God is the moral ruler of the universe, that He will reward the man who forgets Him and will pour misery into the soul of the man who earnestly seeks His face? It is blasphemy to suppose it.

The beasts in the field do not lament that they are not immortal, for they have never had aspirations after immortality. A gracious God has limited their ambition to their attainments. However, if an ox could groan for heaven, or if a sheep could pray for a resurrection, it would be a wretched creature indeed to be denied these things. So the ungodly man, like the beast of the field, has no longing for God's favor, no yearnings for eternal life, no desire to be conformed to the image of Christ. His ambitions are, so far, limited to what he gains.

Is it to be the case that a soul will pant to be like God, will thirst to be reconciled to his Maker, will hunger even to faintness, so that he may find *"peace with God through...Jesus Christ"* (Rom. 5:1), and yet such desires as these are only given to him to make him wretched? I cannot suppose such a thing. The absurdity of imagining that the man who does pray is put in a worse position by God than the man who does not, convinces me that the earnest, faithful prayer will certainly prevail with God through the merit of Christ.

### God is Not the Author of Unnecessary Misery

But I go a step further. Since it is clear that if God does not hear prayer, the praying man would be more wretched than the neglectful sinner, then it would follow that God would be the author of unnecessary misery. Now we know that this is inconsistent with the character of our God. We look around the world, and we see punishment for sin but no punishment for good desires. We discover that the Fall has brought us loss and ruin—and we know that there is a dreadful hell where justice will be executed to the uttermost—but we see no chamber of arbitrary torture where God Almighty takes pleasure in the undeserved pangs and unmerited groans of His own creatures. I do not see a single invention made by God in order to give pain unnecessarily. I do not find a joint of my body, no, not a sinew or a muscle, that is intended to cause me anguish. They may all be racked with aches and pains, since I am a fallen, sinful man, yet the body was not created with a view to pain but for pleasure.

Do you think that God would cunningly put up a mercy seat to increase human misery by a mockery of grace, a mimicry of generosity? Do you dream that He would send out commands to men, obedience to which would confer upon them greater sorrow than disobedience could bring? Do you think that He would woo them with outstretched hands to be more wretched than they were before? Would He be so false and heartless as to bid them to come, knowing that their coming would only make them ten times more unhappy than they were already, because He did not intend to accept them when they did come?

He who can think these things of my God does not know Him. He who could dream that it is possible for Him to invite and incite in you the prayer He has promised to hear, and yet, after all, reject it, must surely be comparing Jehovah to utterly vengeful Hindu gods. He does not know what Jehovah is. Do you not know that prayer itself is the work of God? Prayer is not more the act of created beings than the work of the Creator. Prayer is God in man coming back to God. Prayer is the fruit of divine life. And do you believe that God Himself would write upon the human heart prayers that He did not intend to hear, and that the Spirit would dictate petitions that God the Eternal Father had determined to reject? No, no, no. We must, from this negative way of reasoning, be persuaded that our God will hear and answer prayer.

### God Cannot Be Less Merciful Than Man

If there are still some despairing ones who think that God would invite them to pray and yet reject them, I will put it another way. Would men do so? Would even you, full of sin though you are, so treat your own fellow men? I know that we would hold up to scorn any rich man who would treat beggars in the following way. He would first say to them "I live in such and such a place. It is six miles away. If you will all come tomorrow morning at eight o'clock and knock at my door repeating my son's name, I will supply your needs." And then when he had collected the poor beggars, he would let them stand and knock according to his instructions until they were weary, and never grant them an answer. If he would let them know that there was bread within the house, but not a morsel for them, we would say, "Well, if men must entertain themselves with practical jokes, do not let them be carried out on the poor and needy. Let them find some other victims, and do not let the helpless beggars of the streets be the victims of such foolish mirth."

Is it possible that my God is less generous than men? Do we not find continually that if there is a hospital opened to relieve the sick or to heal the maimed, when many injured people enter in, they are received? I do not know that there is any special amount of compassion in those who have the oversight of the hospital. I do know this, however, that there is so much human kindness in their hearts that, the moment a poor wretch is brought to the door almost dead—if it were a not so serious case they might make some exception—the very desperateness of the case throws open the hospital door, and at once the patient is admitted.

Man is in a similar situation; he is near to death, more than that, condemned and utterly ruined by his sin, and I do not believe that my God will shut His door in the face of misery. I am persuaded that the very desperateness of the case will make an appeal to His heart, and He will fulfill His promise.

This is a poor example, I will admit, for God is infinitely more loving than man. *"As the heavens are higher than the earth, so are* [His] *ways higher than* [our] *ways, and* [His] *thoughts than* [our] *thoughts"* (Isa. 55:9). If a man would not reject the supplication that he himself had invited; if a man's heart would be moved to pity by the cry of misery; much more so will the heart of the all-bounteous God, whose very name is love, and whose nature it is to give liberally without scolding. I am persuaded, therefore, that He must and will hear prayer.

### God Does Not Refuse to Hear Our Prayers

Hearing prayer is God's memorial by which He is distinguished from the false gods. *"They have ears, but they hear not"* (Ps. 115:6). They have hands, but they do not help their worshippers. And they have feet, but they do not come to the rescue of their devotees. Our God made the heavens, and this is His memorial: "The God who hears prayer." Has not David put it: *"O thou that hearest prayer, unto thee shall all flesh come"* (Ps. 65:2)?

One of the standing proofs of the deity of Jehovah is that He does, to this day, answer the supplications of His people. But suppose that you could seek His face day after day, week after week, and month after month, and yet He would refuse you. Where would His memorial be? Oh, if a poor sinner, with tears and plaintive cries, were really to besiege the mercy seat in the name of Jesus, but God the Almighty Father would refuse him and drive him away, I say, where is the name of God that is boasted about?

I grant you, the answer may not come at once, but only so that it may be even more sweet when it comes. I know the ships of heaven may take a long time for their voyage, but only so that they may bring a richer cargo to you; they must come. *"Though* [the vision] *tarry, wait for it; because it will surely come, it will not tarry"* (Hab. 2:3). For otherwise, I say, where is the glory of God? How is He distinguished above Baal? How is He exalted above the gods of the heathen? Did Elijah not put it to the test? The priests of Baal cried. They cut themselves with knives. From morning to evening their shrieks went up to heaven, and the sarcastic prophet said, *"Cry aloud: for he is a god; either he is talking, or he is pursuing, or he is in a journey, or peradventure he sleepeth, and must be awaked"* (1 Kings 18:27).

All day long the knives drew forth priestly blood, but no voice came from Baal. Clear the stage, and let God's servant come. He lifts his hands to heaven and cries:

> LORD *God of Abraham, Isaac, and of Israel, let it be known this day that thou art God in Israel, and that I am thy servant, and that I have done all these things at thy word. Hear me, O* LORD, *hear me, that this people may know that thou art the* LORD *God, and that thou hast turned their heart back again.*
>
> *(1 Kings 18:36–37)*

Down falls the fire of the Lord, consuming not only the bullock, but the stones of the altar and the water in the trench, for our God does hear prayer.

Now do you see that your despair, when you say He will not hear you, really takes away from God one of His grandest titles? You do Him a serious dishonor in supposing that He will refuse to hear you. You throw mud on the insignia of Deity and think unworthily of the Most High when you imagine for an instant that He would teach you to pray and come to Him through the blood of Christ and yet refuse to hear the voice of your groaning.

### God Does Not Make Promises for Nothing

If God does not hear prayer—suppose this to be the case for a moment—then I want to know what is the meaning of His promises. I ask, with all reverence, how will He prove His sincerity, if He does not answer His people? Here are some of His own promises: *"Call upon me in the day of trouble: I will deliver thee, and thou shalt glorify me"* (Ps. 50:15). *"He shall call upon me, and I will answer him"* (Ps. 91:15). And what does this mean, by the mouth of Isaiah: *"He will be very gracious unto thee at the voice of thy cry; when he shall hear it, he will answer thee"* (Isa. 30:19)? That is neither more nor less than a falsehood if God does not hear prayer. What does this splendid passage mean: *"And it shall come to pass, that before they call, I will answer; and while they are yet speaking, I will hear"* (Isa. 65:24)? And what does this verse by Zechariah mean: *"They shall call on my name, and I will hear them: I will say, It is my people: and they shall say, The LORD is my God"* (Zech. 13:9)?

Can there be words plainer than these, from the lips of the Savior?

*Ask, and it shall be given you; seek, and ye shall find; knock, and it shall be opened unto*

18

*you: for every one that asketh receiveth; and he*
*that seeketh findeth; and to him that knocketh*
*it shall be opened....If ye then, being evil, know*
*how to give good gifts unto your children, how*
*much more shall your Father which is in*
*heaven give good things to them that ask him?*
*(Matt. 7:7–8, 11)*

What is the meaning of this great promise: *"And*
*all things, whatsoever ye shall ask in prayer, believ-*
*ing, ye shall receive"* (Matt. 21:22)? Are not all these
promises aimed at the very heart of unbelief?

I will continue with that ancient writing, the
book of Job: *"He shall pray unto God, and he will be*
*favourable unto him: and he shall see his face with*
*joy"* (Job 33:26). The Psalms are crowded with such
promises, and even the prophet Joel, who is full of
thunder and lightning, even he says, *"Whosoever*
*shall call on the name of the LORD shall be delivered"*
(Joel 2:32). The apostle Paul, in the epistle to the
Romans, varies it a little and puts it: *"For whosoever*
*shall call upon the name of the Lord shall be saved"*
(10:13). Even James, who is all practical and not
very comforting, cannot get through his epistle
without saying: *"Draw nigh to God, and he will*
*draw nigh to you"* (4:8). Why, even under the old
law, Deuteronomy had a promise like this: *"If...thou*
*shalt seek the LORD thy God, thou shalt find him, if*
*thou seek him with all thy heart and with all thy*
*soul"* (4:29). Under the laws of the kings, we find it
written: *"If thou seek him, he will be found of thee"*
(1 Chron. 28:9).

I could go on quoting promises until you be-
came weary of such explication. But, my dear

friends, I ask you, if God does not hear prayer, after He has said what I have repeated to you, where is His truthfulness? He must be true, if every man is a liar. His own word must stand, though heaven and earth should pass away. Like flowers, you nations, you will die. Like a dream, you kingdoms, you will melt. Like a shadow, you mountains, you will dissolve. Like a wreck, earth, you will be broken into pieces. Like a worn-out garment, you heavens, you will be rolled up. But every word of God is sure and steadfast. All His promises are Yea and Amen in Christ Jesus (2 Cor. 1:20).

> *The voice said, Cry. And [I] said, What shall I cry? All flesh is grass, and all the goodliness thereof is as the flower of the field: the grass withereth, the flower fadeth...but the word of our God shall stand for ever?* (Isa. 40:6–8)

How can we find arguments stronger than this?

### Jesus' Blood Was Not Shed in Vain

If God has virtually said to us, "Pray, but I will never hear you; seek My face in vain," then I ask, what is the meaning of all the provisions that He has already made for hearing prayer? I see a way to God; it is paved with stones inlaid in the fair crimson of the Savior's blood. I see a door; it is the wounded side of Jesus. Why was that blood shed, if God does not hear prayer? Why was that side torn, if, after all, the veil still shuts us out from access to the mercy seat? Moreover, in heaven I see a Mediator between God and man, but why a Mediator, if God will not be

at peace with man or hear his prayer? In addition, I
see an Intercessor. I see the Son of God stretch His
wounded hands and point to His side. He is wearing
the jeweled breastplate on His forefront; but why is
He wearing the breastplate, and why is He our High
Priest, if prayer is a futile thing and God has said,
*"Seek ye me in vain"*?

Furthermore, I see all the marvelous transactions of the covenant from first to last, and I ask,
why all this, if it is not meant for sinners who seek
His face? Additionally, I see the blessed Spirit; He
Himself condescends to dwell in us and make
*"intercession for us with groanings which cannot be
uttered"* (Rom. 8:26). I ask, you who are melancholy
and despairing, why was this Spirit sent? Why was
this blood shed? Why was this Savior ordained and
exalted on high *"to give repentance...and forgiveness
of sins"* (Acts 5:31) if remission is never to be given,
repentance never to be accepted, and intercession
never to be heard?

By every wound of Jesus, I persuade you, sinner, to believe that God will hear you. By every
drop of that precious blood, by every cry of that
dying lip, by every tear of that weary eye, by every
stinging pain on that bruised back—more than
these—by every jewel in that crown of glory, by
every precious stone upon that priestly breastplate,
by every honor that God the Father has bestowed
upon our Lord Jesus, yes, by all the power of the
blessed Spirit, by all the energy with which He
raised Christ from the dead, by all the power with
which He is acknowledged to be God, I plead with
you never to doubt that God will in due time be
gracious to the voice of your cry.

### Our Preaching Is Not in Vain

Another argument is one that the apostle uses regarding the Resurrection. If God does not hear prayer, what gospel do I have to preach? As the apostle said, concerning the Resurrection, *"Then is our preaching vain, and your faith is also vain....ye are yet in your sins"* (1 Cor. 15:14, 17). If God does not hear prayer, I say, our preaching is vain. We are sent to tell men that *"though your sins be as scarlet, they shall be as white as snow; though they be red like crimson, they shall be as wool"* (Isa. 1:18), if they will turn from their evil ways and seek the Lord. But if they can turn, and yet not be accepted, I, for my part, renounce my commission, for I do not have a gospel that is worth preaching. Surely then you would say, "It is not a gospel worth our acceptance."

If prayer offered in Jesus' name is not accepted, taking Paul's line of argument, then Christ is not accepted. If the sinner's plea, "for Jesus' sake," is not heard, then Christ is not heard. And, if Christ is not heard and accepted, then our preaching is vain and your faith is vain. We are also to be found false witnesses for God, because we have testified of God that He hears the intercession of Jesus—He does not then hear Jesus if He does not hear those who plead Jesus' name. If you could once prove that true prayer could be rejected by God, you have not removed the cornerstone of the Gospel, but you have still taken away a very important building block. And if you could take it away, you would even disturb the keystone of the heavenly arch.

## Comfort to Those Who Seek God

### God Cannot Reject Any Prayer

If any of this could be removed, where is the believer's hope? Hang the heavens in sackcloth, let the sun be turned to darkness, let the moon become a clot of blood, if the mercy seat can be proved to be a mockery. Oh, if God would let His people cry, and not be gracious, it would be better for us if we had never been born! The most happy believer, in his best moment, would be as wretched as the damned in hell, if he were persuaded that God did not, and could not, hear prayer. What would we have to comfort us in our hours of trouble? What would we have to strengthen us in our times of labor? What refuge from the storm? What shelter from the heat? Where, where, could we run, if the throne of grace were a fiction?

Heaven surely would be shut if the gates of prayer were shut. Surely every blessing would pass away at once if prayer ceased to avail. The ladder that Jacob saw would be drawn up into heaven, and henceforth there would be no fellowship between God and man. Glory be to God, such a thing cannot be! Sinner, you think that God would never hurt His saints, but that He would reject you. But see, if He refuses to hear you, the rule is broken, and the rule being once broken, and there being one exception, the whole stability of the saints' comfort is removed with one blow.

### A Soul Cannot Seek the Lord and Be Refused

What would they say in hell, if a soul could really seek the Lord and be refused? Oh, the unholy rejoicing of devils! "Here's a soul," one would say, "who perished even though he prayed. Here's a hand that touched the hem of Jesus' garment, but that garment did not heal. Here are lips, scorched with burning fire, that once were warm with living prayer." I think they would drag such a one in triumph through the streets of hell. They would crowd the thoroughfares to look on, and, oh, what dreadful, scornful applause, what thundering laughter would go up! "Aha! Aha! Aha!" they would say, "Now where is the Savior of whom you boasted? He lied to men's souls. He promised, but He did not give. He taught them to pray, and made them begin their hell on earth, and then threw them into hell forever."

Could it be? Oh, could it be? What would praying men do in hell? I remember a story of Mrs. Ryland, a good Christian woman, who, when she lay dying, was very, very sad, and her husband said to her, "You are dying, my dear?" "Yes," said she. "And where are you going?" he asked. She replied, "Ah! John, I'm going to hell." "And what will you do there?" he said to her. Well, that had not struck her, what she would do there. "Do you think," he inquired, "you will stop praying, Betsy?" "No, John," she said, "even if I were in hell, I would pray." "Oh, but," said he, "they'd say, 'Here's praying Betsy Ryland here. Turn her out; this isn't a fit place for her.'" And so, I think if you could go there with a prayer on your lips, pleading and crying, they would either rejoice over you, as proof that God was not true, or else they would say, "Turn her out. We cannot bear prayers in hell; we could not bear to hear the voice of earnest supplication among the shrieks and curses of lost spirits."

I have been arguing against a thing that you know theoretically is not possible, but yet there are some who, when they are under conviction of sin, still cleave to this dark delusion that God will not hear them. Therefore, I have tried with blow after blow to strike this fear dead, if possible. When Jael did but take one nail and hammer, she was able to smite Sisera through his brain with it. (See Judges 4:17–21.) Since I have used many more nails and have given many more vigorous strokes with the hammer as I could give them, may God make them strong enough to strike the Sisera of unbelief dead at your feet!

## THE POSITIVE

That the Lord does hear prayer, I think may be positively substantiated by the following considerations.

### It Is Consistent with His Nature

Whatever is consistent with God's nature, in the viewpoint of a sound judgment, I believe is true. Now, we cannot perceive any attribute of God that would stand in the way of His hearing prayer. It might be supposed that His justice would, but that has been so satisfied by the Atonement of Christ that it pleads the other way instead. Since Christ has *"put away sin"* (Heb. 9:26), since He has purchased the blessing, it seems only just that God should accept those for whom Jesus died and give the blessing that Christ has bought.

All the attributes of God say to a sinner, "Come, come, come to the throne of grace, and you will have what you want." Omnipotence puts out a strong arm and cries, "I will help you; fear not." Love smiles through bright eyes and cries, *"I have loved thee with an everlasting love: therefore with lovingkindness have I drawn thee"* (Jer. 31:3). Truth speaks in clear, plain language, saying, *"He that seeketh findeth; and to him that knocketh it shall be opened"* (Matt. 7:8). Immutability says, "I am God. I do not change; therefore, you are not consumed." Every single attribute of the divine character—but you can think of these as well as I can—pleads for the man who prays. I do not know of, I never dreamed of, a single divine attribute that could enter an objection. Therefore, I think, if the thing really will glorify God and not dishonor Him, He will certainly do it.

### God Gives to Those Who Least Deserve It

"Oh, but," you say, "I am such a great sinner!" To give to a man what he deserves is not charity. To bestow a favor upon those who have a little offended is no very great act of charity. But, to choose out the biggest rebel in His dominions and to say to that rebel, "I forgive you," yes, to take that rebel and to adopt him into His family, adorn him with jewels, and set a crown of gold upon his head, is this the manner of men, O Lord God? No, it is in such cases that we see the broad distinction between the leniency of human sovereigns and the mighty sovereign grace that is in the King of Kings.

The worse you make your case out to be, the better is my argument. The worse the disease, the more credit to the physician who heals. The worse the sin, the more glory to the astounding mercy that puts it away. The greater the rebel, the more triumphant the grace that makes that rebel into a child. I say that the greatness of your sin may act as a foil to set forth the brightness of God's love. And in this, because hearing your unworthy prayers and listening to the cry that comes out of your polluted lips would honor Him, I am persuaded He will do it.

### It Is Harmonious with God's Past Actions

If you want a history of God's dealings with men, turn to Psalm 107. There you find travelers lost, like you, in a desert. They wander in a wilderness in a solitary way; they find no city to dwell in. The water in the bottle is used up; the bread that was carried on the camels' backs is all gone; and they find no well. They perceive no way, and they follow this path, then that. At last, hungry and thirsty, their souls faint within them, and up from the desert's parched sand there arises to the burning sky the voice of wailing: "O God, spare us, and let us live." How is it written? *"He delivered them out of their distresses. And he led them forth by the right way, that they might go to a city of habitation"* (vv. 6–7). For the Scripture says, *"he satisfieth the longing soul, and filleth the hungry soul with goodness"* (v. 9).

This is not told to us as the exception, but as the rule. This is God's way of dealing with men. When they are lost and turn to Him, He hears them. "Ah!" you say, "I am lost, but I am not like those travelers. I am lost by reason of my own sin." The next case in this psalm will fit your situation. Here we find rebels brought into prison. They have been rebelling against the Word of God, and they have despised the counsel of the Most High; therefore, He brought them down by labor. They fell down, and there were none to help them. Then they cried to God in their trouble. Did He hear them? These were rebels, appropriately and properly put in prison, justly and rightly fettered with irons. Do you wear the fetters of conscience and the chains of terror? Are you in the prison of the law? So long as you are not in the final prison house of hell, if you call upon God in your trouble, you will find that it will be with you as it was with them. *"He brought them out of darkness and the shadow of death, and brake their bands in sunder"* (v. 14).

"Oh, but," says another, "I have gotten into trouble through my sin, but I do not know how to pray as I should. I am such a stupid person!" Then the next case is yours. *"Fools because of their transgression, and because of their iniquities, are afflicted"* (v. 17). One of these *"fools"* had brought on disease by his sin, and he was so painfully sick that he lost all his appetite. He abhorred all kinds of food and drew near to the gates of death. What sort of prayer did this fool pray? Why, a fool's prayer, certainly, but God will hear a fool's prayer, as it is written, *"He sent his word, and healed them, and delivered them from their destructions"* (v. 20). So, if you are ever as great a fool as this, and the suffering you now feel has been brought on you through your own folly, He will still hear you.

"Ah, but," you say, "I have been such a bragging fellow, such a boaster, and I have done such terrible deeds in my day!" What is the next case? The case of the sailor. You know, we generally think that seafaring men do not care about much. They are daredevils and throw out curse words without remorse. In the past, I imagine, they were worse than they are now, so that when they did get ashore, they were a true example of everything mischievous and bad. But in this psalm we have a crew of sailors in a storm. They had, no doubt, been cursing and swearing in the calm, but now there is a storm. Their ship rises into the air, and then it goes down again into the depths: *"They reel to and fro, and stagger like a drunken man"* (v. 27), for they cannot walk across the deck. The ship reels; they *"are at their wit's end"* (v. 27), and they think, "Surely she will go to the bottom." Then they cry to God. There was no chaplain on board. Who prayed? Why, the boatswain and the captain and the crew, and I think it is likely that they did not know how to put the words together. They were more used to swearing than to praying, but they went down on their knees on deck, clinging to the mast and bulwark and tiller. They cried, "O God! O God! Save us. The water is swallowing us up. God of the storm, deliver us."

Did He hear the sailors' prayer—the frantic cry of sinking men? Read here: *"He maketh the storm a calm, so that the waves thereof are still. Then are they glad because they be quiet; so he bringeth them unto their desired haven"* (vv. 29–30). Well now, you who have been accustomed to cursing and swearing, and who say, "What is the use of my praying?" here is a case that just suits you. And this is the rule, I say again, not the exception, and I argue, therefore, from the past acts and ways of God, that He will now hear your prayer.

### God Must Hear Prayer Because of His Promises

God is free, but His promises bind Him. God may do as He wills, but He always wills to do what He has said He will do. We have no claim upon God, but God makes a claim for us. When He gives a promise, we may confidently plead it. I venture to say that promises made in Scripture are God's commitments, and that as no honorable man ever runs back from his commitments, so a God of honor and a God of truth cannot, from the necessity of His nature, allow one of His words to fall to the ground. All of God's promises can be found in the Bible. Only *"let God be true, but every man a liar"* (Rom. 3:4). If God promises something, He must and will perform it, or else He would not be true.

### We Must Decide for Ourselves

While I dare to say that the fact that God answers prayer is certified by an abundance of facts in my own experience, I observe that the best proof is for you to try it for yourself. It is said that there is no way to learn to ride a horse except on a horse's back, and I believe there is no way to learn any truth except by experiencing it. If you want to know the depravity of the human heart, you must find it out when you look at your daily imperfections, and if you want to know that God hears prayer, you must test the fact, for you will never learn it through my saying, "He heard me." You will only know it through His having heard you. I would, therefore, exhort you, since it is not a possibility, a chance, or a maybe, but since it is a dead—I must not use that word—since it

30

is a living certainty that *"every one that asketh receiveth; and he that seeketh findeth"* (Matt. 7:8), to fall on your knees and pray to God. Pray to Him even now to save your soul.

Ambition tempts you to disappointment. Riches draw you to risky business transactions that will lead to failure. Your own passions drive you to pleasures that end in pain. The best the world can promise you is a perhaps, but my Master presents to you *"the sure mercies of David"* (Isa. 55:3)—certainties, infallible certainties. Will you not have them? Oh, may the Spirit of God lead you to accept them.

In your room you may pray; wherever you are, the silent cry may go up to heaven. In the factory or the garden or the field or the street or the prison cell—wherever you have a heart to pray, God has an ear to hear. No words are needed, except those that spring spontaneously to your lips. Tell Him you are a wretch, that you are undone without His sovereign grace. Tell Him you have no hope in yourself. Tell Him you have no merits; tell Him you cannot save yourself. Say, "Lord, save, or I perish!" That was Peter's sinking prayer, but it preserved him from drowning. Say, *"God be merciful to me a sinner"* (Luke 18:13). That was the publican's prayer in the temple; it justified him.

Bring a suffering Savior before a gracious God. Point to the wounds of Jesus, and say, "Oh, God, though my heart is as hard as a millstone, Christ's heart was broken. Though my conscience is callous and not tender, the flesh of Christ was tender, and it stung painfully. Though I can give no atonement, Christ gave it; though I bring no merits, I plead the merits of Jesus."

And let me say to you, pray as if you meant it, and continue as Elijah did, until you get the blessing. I pray to God that some of you will never rise from your knees until God has heard you. Plead with Him as a man pleads for his life. Clutch the horns of the altar as a drowning man clutches the life preserver. Lay hold of God, as Jacob grasped the angel, and do not let Him go until He blesses you, for *"thus saith the LORD...I have not spoken in secret, in a dark place of the earth: I said not unto the seed of Jacob, Seek ye me in vain"* (Isa. 45:18–19).

## Chapter 2

## Finding the Light

*"We wait for light, but behold obscurity; for
brightness, but we walk in darkness."*
—Isaiah 59:9

Israel had greatly revolted from her God, and in consequence she had brought upon herself great sorrow. Still, instead of repenting of their faults and returning to their allegiance to Jehovah, the people of this nation continued to be duped by false prophets and presumptuous pride into the expectation of better days. The better days did not come. They looked for the sunshine, but they wandered in the mists. They waited for brightness, but walked in gloom. Unhappy Israel!

She turned aside from Jehovah to worship Baal. She went after the gods of the heathen, which were no gods, and from that hour her land was afflicted with pestilence and famine. The spoiler came up against her. He stopped her wells, cut down her vines, and stripped the bark from her fig trees. In the end, he carried her away captive and caused the sons and daughters of Zion to sit down by the waters of Babylon and weep at the remembrance of the beloved city (Ps. 137:1).

Sin is always a bitter thing, and they who follow it, expecting to arrive at the light of joy, are duped and deceived. They will be plunged into denser and denser darkness until they arrive at an unending midnight, which is never broken by a solitary star. This historical example might be used by way of warning to any who seek happiness and who foolishly expect to find it in the pleasures of sin and in neglecting God. You will certainly be disappointed, for "joy is a plant that does not grow on nature's barren soil." Only a renewed nature can be blessed.

The more intensely you pursue happiness in the bewitching path of sin, the further will it fly from you. Like the will-o'-the-wisp, the glare of pleasure will entice you into the quagmire, but it will leave you there to find that your chase has gained you nothing but danger and weariness. The pearl of happiness does not lie in the depths of dissipation. The broad road always ends in destruction, never in peace. You may hoist the sails of desire to the breeze, let go of the helm of reason, and let your soul be conveyed wherever the blasts of temptation or the currents of custom may direct. One thing you may make sure of, your unhappy ship will never be carried by such means into the haven of peace. Such a voyage will certainly end in shipwreck.

Disappointment is attached in the same manner to other ways of living. It is vain to pile up gold. It is vain to awaken the trumpet call of fame. It is vain to gather learning or to master eloquence, eminence, rank, wealth, and power. All these things are too little to satisfy the insatiable craving of an immortal soul. You must have God or you will never have enough. You must be reconciled to Him, or you can never be at peace with yourself. You must enter into a covenant of peace with God, or all the creatures of God will conspire against you. Pilgrim of earth, your way must be towards holiness and God, or in vain you will expect the daylight to dawn. To the sinner, the blackness of darkness is reserved forever, and even now his way is hard and his path darkened with fear and anxiety.

However, I now want to apply the words of the Scripture text to another group of people: those who are sincerely seeking better things, who want to obtain the true and heavenly light. They have waited, hoping to receive it; but instead of obtaining it, they are in a worse, at least in a sadder, state than they were. They almost have been driven into the dark apprehension that for them no light will ever come, and they will be prisoners chained forever in the valley of the shadow of death. If God will bless a few words of awakening and encouragement to such prisoners, so that some will see the heavenly light, my heart will be much happier.

## QUALITIES OF THOSE WHO SEEK

### They Are Aware of Their Natural Darkness

According to the text, these people are looking for light. They are not content with their obscurity; they are waiting for brightness. Out of those who are reading this, there are a few who are not content to be what their first birth has made them. They discover in their nature much evil that they would be glad to be rid of. They find in their understanding much ignorance, and they would be glad to be illuminated. They do not understand the Scripture when they read it, and though they hear gospel terms, they fail to grasp gospel thought.

They desire to escape from this ignorance. They desire to know the truth that saves the soul, and their desire is not only to know it in theory, but to know it by its practical power upon their inner man. They are truly and anxiously desirous to be delivered from the sinful nature, which they believe to be a dangerous one, and to be brought into the glorious liberty of the children of God.

Oh, but the best of hearers are these in whom right desires have begun to be awakened. Men who are dissatisfied with the darkness are evidently not altogether dead, for the dead will slumber in the catacombs, heedless of whether it is noon or night. They ask for no sunbeams to molest their dreams, because people sleep better because of the darkness. The men who do not so desire the darkness are evidently not altogether asleep, and they are evidently not altogether blind, for to the blind it does not matter much whether the sun floods the landscape with glory or night conceals it with a black veil.

Those who are looking for light are evidently somewhat awakened, aroused, and stirred. This is no small blessing, for, alas, most people are an apathetic mass regarding spiritual things. I might as easily strive to create a soul within the ribs of death, or call forth warm tears of pity from marble, as to evoke spiritual emotions from the people of this generation. Therefore, the people whom I seek to address are in a hopeful condition, for as the trees twist their branches towards the sunlight, these people long for Jesus, the light and life of all people. Moreover, they have a high idea of what the light is. In the text they call it *"brightness."* They wait for it and are grieved because it does not come.

If you greatly value spiritual light, my dear friend, you are under no misapprehension. If you consider it to be a priceless thing to obtain an interest in Christ, the forgiveness of your sins, and peace with God, you are using sober judgment. You will never exaggerate in your estimation of the one thing that is needed. It is true that those who trust in God are a happy people. It is true that to be brought into sonship and adopted into the family of the great God is a favor for which kings might well exchange their crowns.

You cannot think too highly of the blessings of grace. I would rather incite in you a sacred covetousness after them than by the remotest degree lower your estimate of their preciousness. Salvation is such a blessing that heaven hangs upon it. If you gain grace, you have the seed of heaven within you, the security, the pledge of everlasting bliss. Therefore, if you are looking for the light, there are many hopeful signs in you. It is well that you loathe the darkness and prize the light.

### They Have Hope That They May Obtain This Light

People who are waiting for this light are waiting in hope and are somewhat disappointed that, after waiting for the light, darkness has come. They are evidently astonished at the failure of their hopes. They are amazed to find themselves walking in darkness when they had fondly hoped that the candle of the Lord would shine around about them. My dear friend, I want to encourage in you that spark of hope, for despair is one of the most terrible hindrances to the reception of the Gospel. As long as awakened sinners cherish a hope of mercy, there is hope for them.

I hope, seeker, that before long you will be able to sing of pardon bought with blood, and when the scene of life is over, that you will enter through the gates into the pearly city and live among the blessed who forever see the face of the Well Beloved. Though it may seem too good to be true, even you, in your calmer moments, envision that one day you will rejoice that Christ is yours and take your seat among His people, though you are the lowest of them all in your own estimation. Then you imagine in your heart how fervently you will love your Redeemer, how rapturously you will kiss the very dust of His feet, how gratefully you will bless Him who has lifted the poor from the dunghill and caused them to sit among princes. How I long to see this hope of yours transformed into joyful reality. May the chosen hour strike at this present moment. May you no longer look through the window wistfully at the banquet, but come in to sit at the table and feed upon Christ, rejoicing with His chosen.

### They Have Learned to Plead Their Cases with God

Our text is a complaint addressed to the Lord Himself. *"We wait for light, but behold obscurity; for brightness, but we walk in darkness."* It is a declaration of inward feelings, a laying bare of hearts' agonies to the Most High. Ah, dear friend, although you have not yet found the peace you seek, it is well that you have begun to pray. Perhaps you think your prayers are inadequate. Indeed, you hardly dare to call it prayer at all, but God does not judge as you do. A groan is heard in heaven; a deep sigh and a falling tear are prevalent weapons at the throne of God.

Yes, your soul cries to God, and you cannot help it. When you are about your daily work, you find yourself sighing, "Oh, if only my load of guilt were gone. If only I could call the Lord my Father with an unfaltering tongue!" Night after night and day after day this desire rises from you like the morning mist from the valleys. Right now, you would tear off your right arm and pluck out your right eye if you could only gain the unspeakable blessing. You are sincerely anxious for reconciliation with God, and your anxiety reveals itself in prayer and supplication. I hope these prayers will continue. I trust you will never cease crying out to God. May the Holy Spirit compel you to continue to sigh and groan. Like the persistent woman, may you press your suit until the gracious answer is granted, through the merits of Jesus.

If you are looking for light and praying persistently, dear friend, things are hopeful with you, but when I say hopeful, I wish I could say much more, for mere hopefulness is not enough. It is not enough to desire, it is not enough to seek, it is not enough to pray; you must actually obtain; you must truly lay hold of eternal life. You will never enjoy comfort and peace until you have moved from the merely hopeful stage into a better and a brighter one, by making sure of your share in the Lord Jesus by a living, appropriating faith. In the exalted Savior, all the gifts and graces that you lack are stored up in readiness to supply your needs. Oh, may you come to His fullness, and out of it receive grace for grace.

### They Are Willing to Expose Their Hearts Before God

People like those in our text are willing to confess their desires, whether right or wrong, and to expose their conditions, whether unhealthy or sound. When we try to cloak anything from God, we are both wicked and foolish. When we have a desire to hide away from our Maker, it indicates that we have a rebellious spirit. But when a man uncovers his wound, invites inspection of it, bids the surgeon to cut away the scaly film that covered its infection, and says to him, "Here, probe into its depths, see what is harmful in it. Do not spare anything, but make sure that the wound will heal," then he has a good chance of recovery. When a man is willing to make God his confessor, and freely and without hypocrisy pours out his heart like water before the Lord, there is good hope for him.

I believe that many reading this may be in this situation. You have told the Lord your case; you have spread your petitions before Him. I trust you will continue to do so until you find relief, but I have a still higher hope, namely, that you may soon obtain peace with God through Jesus Christ our Lord.

### ERRORS OF THOSE WHO SEEK

It is now my happy task to endeavor to assist into the light those who are willing to flee from the darkness. I will do so by trying to answer these questions: "Since I desire the light, why have I not found it yet? Why am I left to grope like a blind man for the wall, and stumble at noon as in the night? Why has the Lord not revealed Himself to me?"

## Seeking in the Wrong Place

Many, like Mary, seek the living among the dead. It is possible that you may have been the victim of the false doctrine that peace with God can be found in the use of rituals. It may be that you have been taught by that church that vainly rests its faith on the fallacy of apostolic succession and the empty parade of the ordination of bishops. You have been taught to believe in regeneration by baptism and confirmation by the laying on of hands. You have been deceived by the dogma of the importance of sacraments and the power of the priesthood. If so, it is little wonder that you have not found peace, for, believe me, there is no peace to be found in the whole round of rituals, even if they were those that God Himself prescribed.

There is no peace to be found in such ceremonies, except the deadly peace that rocks souls who are in the cradle of superstition into that deep sleep from which only the trumpet of Judgment will awaken them. It is they who receive a strong delusion to believe a lie so that they all may be damned. May you, my reader, escape from so terrible a doom. God has never promised salvation through the use of ceremonies. The Gospel that He sent His servants to preach was never a gospel of postures, genuflections, symbols, and rituals. The Gospel is revealed in these words: *"Believe on the Lord Jesus Christ, and thou shalt be saved"* (Acts 16:31)—a mental thing, a spiritual thing, an inner thing, but not at all an outward

41

display, a matter of the senses and the flesh. Our Gospel is altogether a matter for heart and soul and spirit. And your salvation must be such, or you can never be saved.

It is possible, dear friend, that you have been looking for salvation by merely believing a certain creed. You have thought that if you could discover pure orthodoxy and could then conform your soul to its mold, you would be saved. You have consequently believed unreservedly, as far as you have been able to do so, the set of truths that have been handed to you by the tradition of your ancestors. It may be that your creed is Calvinistic, it is possible that it is Arminian, it may be Protestant, it may be Roman Catholic, it may be truth, it may be a lie; but, believe me, solid peace with God is not to be found through the mere reception of any creed, however true or scriptural. Mere head knowledge is not the road to heaven. *"Ye must be born again"* (John 3:7) means a great deal more than that you must believe certain dogmas.

It is of the utmost possible importance, I grant you, that you should search the Scriptures. Yet the study of these, good as it is, cannot save you. You think you have eternal life in them, but recollect how our Lord reprimanded the Pharisees. He told them that even though they searched the Scriptures, they did not accept that the Scriptures testified about Him. He added, *"Ye will not come to me, that ye might have life"* (John 5:40). Have you stopped short at the Scriptures, and therefore short of eternal life? You must press beyond this. You must come to the living, personal Christ, once crucified but now living to plead at the right hand of God, or else your acceptance of the soundest creed cannot avail for the salvation of your soul.

You may be misled in some other manner, or some other mistaken way of seeking peace may have deceived you. If so, I pray to God that you may see the mistake and understand that there is but one door to salvation, and that is Christ. There is one way, and that is Christ; one truth, and that is Christ; one life, and that is Christ. Salvation lies in Jesus only. It does not lie in you, in what you do, what you feel, what you know, or what you resolve. In Him all life and light for the sons of men are stored up by the mercy of God the Father. One reason why you have not found the light may be because you have sought it in the wrong place.

### Seeking in the Wrong Spirit

My dear friend, when we ask for pardon, reconciliation, salvation, we must remember to whom we speak. When we ask for favor, we must also remember who we are. Some appear to deal with God as if He were obligated to give salvation, as if salvation indeed were the inevitable result of a round of performances or the deserved reward of a certain amount of virtue. They refuse to see that salvation is a pure gift of God, not of works. It is not the result of merit, but of free favor only, not of man, or by man, but of the Lord alone. Though the Lord has placed it on record in His Word, in the plainest language, that *"it is not of him that willeth, nor of him that runneth, but of God that showeth mercy"* (Rom. 9:16), most men in their hearts imagine that everlasting life is tied to duties and earned by service.

Dear friend, you must come down from such arrogant notions. You must appeal for your pardon as a poor person. You must come before God as a humble petitioner, pleading the promises of mercy, abhorring all idea of merit, confessing that if the Lord condemns you He has a right to do it, and that if He saves you, it will be an act of pure, gratuitous mercy, a deed of sovereign grace. Oh, but too many of you seekers hold your heads too high. You must stoop to enter the lowly gate of light. The penitent's true place is on bended knee. *"God be merciful to me a sinner"* (Luke 18:13) is the true prayer of someone who is repentant.

Why, if God should condemn you, you could never complain of injustice, for you have deserved it a thousand times, and if those prayers of yours were never answered, if no mercy ever came, you could not accuse the Lord, for you have no right to be heard. He could righteously withhold an answer of peace if He willed to do so. Confess that you are an undeserving, punishment-deserving, hell-deserving sinner, and begin to pray as you have never before prayed. Cry out of the depths of self-abasement if you want to be heard. Come as a beggar, not as a creditor. Come to earnestly implore, not to demand. Use only this argument, "Lord, hear me, for You are gracious, and Jesus died. I cry to You as a condemned criminal who seeks pardon. Deliver me from going down into the pit so that I may praise Your name."

This harboring of a proud spirit, I fear, may have been a great source of harm for many of you, and if it has been so, amend it, I implore you. Go now with humble and contrite hearts, in lowliness and brokenness of spirit, to your Father whom you have offended, for He will surely accept you as His children.

## Seeking Without Understanding the Way to Find Peace

Even though the way to peace with God is often explained, it is not understood very well by many. They have a hazy comprehension of it, that even if you explain it very clearly, they will, if it is possible, misunderstand you. Dear reader, your salvation does not depend upon what you do, but upon what Christ did almost two thousand years ago when He offered Himself as a sacrifice for sin. Your salvation takes root in the death agonies of Calvary. There the great Substitute truly bore your sin and suffered its penalty. Your sin will never destroy you if upon that bloody tree the Lord's chosen High Priest made a full atonement for your sins. They will not be laid against you anymore forever.

The only thing you have to do is to accept what Jesus has finished. I know that your idea of salvation is that you are to bring something to Him, but that boastful idea has ruined many and will ruin more. When you will finally come empty-handed, and be willing to accept a free and full salvation from the hand of the Crucified, then, and then only, will you be saved. "There is life for a look at the Crucified One."

But men will not look to the Cross. No, they conspire to raise another cross, or they aspire to adorn that cross with jewels or sweet flowers. But they will not give a simple look to the Savior and rely alone on Him. Yet, dear reader, no soul can ever obtain peace with God by any other means. This means is so effective that it never has failed and never will. As in the story of Elisha and Naaman, the waters of Abana and Pharpar are preferred by proud human nature, but the waters of Jordan alone can take away the leprosy.

Our repenting, our doing, our resolving, are just *"broken cisterns,"* but the only drink of life is to be found in the *"fountain of living waters"* (Jer. 2:13), opened up by our Immanuel's death. Do you understand that a simple trust, a sincere dependence, a hearty reliance upon Christ, is the way of salvation? If you know this, may the God who taught You to understand the way, give you grace to run in it, for then your light has come. Arise and shine. Your peace has come, for Christ has bought it with His blood. He has been punished for all who trust in Him. Their sins are gone:

> Lost as in a shoreless flood,
> Drown'd in the Redeemer's blood;
> Pardon'd soul, how bless'd art thou,
> Justified from all things now!

### Seeking in a Half-Hearted Manner

None enter heaven who are only half inclined to go there. Cold prayers ask God to refuse them. When a man manifestly does not value the mercy for which he asks and would be perfectly content not to receive it, it is small wonder if he is denied. Many a sinner lies freezing outside the door of God's mercy for years because he has never thoroughly stirred himself to take the kingdom of heaven with zeal. If you can by any means be made willing to remain unsaved, you will be left to perish, but if you are inwardly set and resolved that you will give God no rest until you win a pardon from Him, He will give you your heart's desire. The man who must be saved will be. The man whose heart is set to find the way to Zion's hill, will find that way.

I believe that a sense of our pardon usually comes to us when, Samson-like, we grasp the posts of mercy's door with desperate vehemence as though we would pull them up, post and bar and all, rather than remain any longer shut out from peace and safety. Strong imploring and tears, groanings of spirit, vehement longings, and ceaseless pleadings— these are the weapons that win us the victory in our warfare of seeking the Lord through the blood of Jesus. Perhaps, then, my dear friend, you have not stirred yourself as you should have. May the Lord help you to be a mighty wrestler and then a prevailing prince.

### Seeking while Harboring Some Sin

To bring this subject home to your conscience: is it not possible, is it not rather fearfully probable, that there may be some sin within you that you are harboring, to your soul's peril? When a soldier's foot has refused to heal, the surgeon has been known to examine it very minutely and manipulate every part. Each bone is there and in its place. There is no apparent cause for the inflammation, but yet the wound refuses to heal. The surgeon probes and probes again until his scalpel comes into contact with a hard foreign substance. "Here it is," he says, "a bullet is lodged here. This must come out or the wound will never close." In the same way, my probe, dear reader, may discover a secret in you, and if so, it must come out, or you must die.

You cannot expect to have peace with God and still indulge in that drunkard's glass. What, a drunkard reconciled to God? You cannot hope to enjoy peace with God and yet refuse to speak with that relative who offended you years ago. What, look to be forgiven when you yourself will not forgive? You have doubtful business practices in your trade. Do you dare to hope that God will accept a thief? For that is what you are, a thief and a liar. You label your goods dishonestly, charging them twenty instead of fifteen. Do you expect God to be your friend while you remain a cheat? Do you think He will smile on you in your deceit and walk with you when you choose dirty ways? Perhaps you indulge a haughty spirit, or it may be an idle disposition. It does not matter much which kind of devil is in you, it must come out or else the peace of God cannot come in.

Now, are you willing to give sin up? If not, it is all a waste of time for me to tell you of Christ, for He is not meant to be a Savior of those who persevere in sin. He came to save His people *from* their sins, not *in* them, and if you still must cling to a favorite sin, do not be deceived, for you can never enter within the gates of heaven.

### Seeking Only Occasionally

During an earnest sermon you have been awakened, but when the sermon has concluded, you have gone back to your slumber like the sluggard who turns over on his side to sleep some more. After a sickness, or when there has been a death in the family, you have then zealously stirred yourself, but later you have fallen into the same carelessness as before. Oh, fool that you are, remember that he who runs by spurts does not win the race, but he who continues running to the end, wins. He who thinks of Christ now and then, and in the meantime regards vanity and falsehood in his heart, does not receive Him. He who must have Christ, who must have Him now, and who gives his whole heart to Him and cries, "I will seek Him until I find Him, and when I find Him I will never let Him go," alone will have Him.

### Seeking while Being Disobedient to the Gospel Principle

A great reason that earnest souls do not find rest quickly is that they do not follow this essential gospel principle: *"Believe on the Lord Jesus Christ, and thou shalt be saved"* (Acts 16:31). It is not necessary at all to combat their doubts and fears; I may do it, but I do not know that I am called upon to do so.

Now, if this is the case with you, the plain matter of fact is, God lays down a way of peace, and you will not have it. God says that if you believe in Jesus you will live. You will not believe in Christ, and yet you hope to live! God reveals to you His dear Son and says, "Trust Him," and moreover says, *"He that believeth not God hath made him a liar"* (1 John 5:10), and yet you dare to make God a liar. Every minute that you live in a state of unbelief, you, so far

as you can, make God to be a liar! What an atrocity
for any of us to fall into! What an amazing presumption for a sinner who professes to be seeking peace
with God to live in!

Oh, hear me now, I beg you. I will trade my soul
for your soul, if you are not saved today by trusting
in the work of Jesus Christ. If you do not find eternal life in Jesus, then all believers also must perish
with you, for this is our hope, our only hope, and if it
fails you, it will also fail us. Therefore, with confidence, knowing they cannot fail any of us, I declare
to you these faithful sayings, which are worthy of all
understanding: *"Christ Jesus came into the world to
save sinners"* (1 Tim. 1:15), even the chief. *"He that
believeth on the Son hath everlasting life"* (John
3:36). *"Believe on the Lord Jesus Christ, and thou
shalt be saved"* (Acts 16:31), for *"he that believeth
and is baptized shall be saved; but he that believeth
not shall be damned"* (Mark 16:16).

## ENCOURAGEMENT FOR THOSE WHO SEEK

My dear friend, I am imagining that I am
searching your eyes intently. I fear for you; I am
afraid you will become frostbitten by your long sorrow and fall into a fatal slumber. You have been
seeking rest, but you have not found it. What an unhappy state you are in! You are not now reconciled
to God. Your sin clamors for punishment. You are
among those with whom God is angry every day. Can
you bear to be in such a condition? Does something
not warn you to arise and flee out of this city of destruction, for fear that you will be consumed? What
happiness you are missing every day!

If you will lay hold of Christ by faith, you will possess a joy and peace that are beyond all understanding. You are fretting in this low and miserable dungeon. You have been in the dark year after year, when the sun is shining, the sweet flowers are blooming, and everything is waiting to lead you forth with gladness. Oh, what joys you lose by being an unbeliever! Why do you remain for so long in this evil state? Meanwhile, what good you might have done! Oh, if you had been led to look to Jesus Christ many months ago, instead of sitting in darkness, you would have been leading others to Christ and pointing other eyes to that dear Cross that brought peace to you.

What sin you are daily committing, for you are daily an unbeliever, daily treating the precious blood with contempt, daily denying the ability of Christ, and so doing injury to His honor. Does not the Spirit of God within you make you say, *"I will arise and go to my father"* (Luke 15:18)? Oh, if there is such a thought trembling in your soul, do not quench it. Obey it, arise and go, and may your Father's arms be around your neck before this day's sun goes down.

Meanwhile, dear friend, permit me to say what a hardening process is going on within you of which you are unconscious! If you are not better, you are certainly worse than you were twelve months ago. Why, those promises that encouraged you then now bring you no comfort! Those threats that once startled you now cause you no alarm! Will you wait longer? You have waited to be better, and you are growing worse and worse. You have said, "I will come at a more convenient time," and every season is more inconvenient than that which came before it.

You doubted then; you are the victim of deeper and more cowardly doubts today.

Oh, if only you could believe in Him who must be true. Oh, if only you could trust in Him who ought to be trusted, for He can never deceive. I pray to God that the day will come, that it will come even now at this very moment, when you may shake yourself from the dust and arise and put on your beautiful garments. For every hour that you sit on the dunghill of your soul-destroying doubts, you are being fastened by strong bands of iron to the seat of despair. Your eye is growing dimmer, your hand more palsied, and the poison in your veins is raging more furiously. Nearby is the Savior's cross, and there is potency in His blood for you. Trust Jesus now, and at this moment you will enter into peace. The gate of mercy swings readily on its hinge and opens wide to every soul who casts itself on the heart of the Savior. Oh, why do you wait? Evil will come to you. The sun is going down. Hurry traveler, or you will be overtaken with an everlasting night.

What else can I say to arouse you but this: every man and every woman reading this who is unconverted, however hopeful they may be, is running the awful risk of sinking into the place where hope does not come! As the Lord my God lives, with all the hopefulness that is now around you, unless you believe in Jesus, you will be condemned. There may be ten thousand good points about you, but if you miss this one, you must be an outcast. My soul is grieved and troubled within me that I have such a message to deliver, but I must speak plainly.

Will you have Christ or not? If not, then, whatever you may glory in, Christ will not know you in the Day of His coming, but you will hear Him say, "Depart from Me, I never knew you." Unless Jesus Christ is your shield and help, you are undone. But you may have Him; you may have Him now. His Spirit speaks through my words to you at this time. I know He does. You are feeling even now the gentle motions of His mighty power.

> Yield to his love who round you now
> The bands of a man would cast,
> The cords of his love, who was given for you,
> To his altar binding you fast.

This is your only opportunity. When your life is over, Christ will not be preached in hell; the Gospel will not be proclaimed amid the flames of hades. Perhaps, for some of you, even this day is your only day of grace. Now your conscience is still tender. Tomorrow, touched by that hot iron, which Satan always has at hand, your conscience may become seared, never to feel again. Now the gospel trumpet sounds sweet and clear, "Come and welcome, come and welcome, come and welcome, sinners, come." Your guilt will vanish completely away, even though it was as black as hell before. All things that separate you and God will be removed. Only trust in Jesus, and you will live. I wish to put it to you more powerfully, but I cannot. There is the Gospel. You have heard it now. Perhaps you will never hear it again, or, if you do hear it again, perhaps it will never have the power to draw you as it has at this time.

By the wounds of Christ, I pray that you will not turn from Him. By the second coming of Christ, I pray that you will regard Him! Since He will shortly descend in the clouds of heaven to call the nations to account, I pray that you will bow to Him! By that pierced hand that will sway the scepter, by those weeping eyes that will flash like flames of fire, by those lips of mercy that will pronounce sentences of thunder to be accompanied with an execution of lightning, I pray that you will *"kiss the Son, lest he be angry, and ye perish from the way, when his wrath is kindled but a little"* (Ps. 2:12)! I tell you of Christ with the crown of thorns, Christ with the wounded hands, Christ with the opened side, who is full of tenderness and mercy to sinners, though they forget Him and neglect Him. But if You will not have this Christ, then I must tell you of the Christ who will come:

> With the rainbow wreath and robes of storm,
> On cherub wings and wings of wind,
> Appointed Judge of all mankind.

You may reject Him today, but you will not escape Him then. You may turn your back on Him on this day, but the mountains will refuse to give you shelter in that tremendous hour. Come, bow at His feet. Look up now to His dear face and say, "I trust You, Jesus, I trust You now. Save me now, for I am vile."

## COME TO JESUS

Dear friends, there are many, many around you, some of whom you know, who have trusted Jesus, and they have found light. They once suffered your disappointments, but they have now found rest for their souls. They came to Jesus just as they were, and at this moment they can tell you that they are satisfied in Him. If others have found such peace, why not you? Jesus is still the same. It is not to Christ's advantage to reject a sinner. It is not to God's glory to destroy a seeker; rather, it is to His honor and glory to receive those who humbly rest in the sacrifice of His dear Son. What holds you back? You are called; come. You are urged to come; come.

In the courts of law, I have sometimes heard a man called as a witness. As soon as he is called, even though he may be at the back of the courtroom, he begins to press his way up to the witness box. Nobody says, "Who is this man pushing here?" or, if they were to say, "Who are you?" it would be a sufficient answer to say, "My name was called." "But you are not rich, you have no gold ring on your finger!" "No, but that is not the point, I was called." "But you are not a man of fame or rank or character!" "It does not matter; I was called. Make way." So make way, you doubts and fears; make way, you devils of the infernal lake; Christ calls the sinner. Sinner, come. Even though you have nothing to recommend you, it is written, *"Him that cometh to me I will in no wise cast out"* (John 6:37). Therefore, come, and the Lord will bless you, for Christ's sake.

# Chapter 3

## "Seeking for Jesus"

*When the people therefore saw that Jesus was not there, neither his disciples, they...came to Capernaum, seeking for Jesus.*
—John 6:24

The persons who are described in our text as *"seeking for Jesus"* were looking for Him from a very base and selfish motive, not because of the gracious words that He spoke or to give Him thanks for benefits received at His hands. They were seeking merely because they had eaten of the loaves and fishes and hoped to do so again. Let us flee from such sordid motives. May we shun with revulsion the very idea of making a profession of religion for the sake of worldly advantage. It is detestable to the last degree. Those who seek Jesus Christ with the groveling desire to pursue godliness for their own personal profit are hypocrites of the lowest order. Like Judas, they will follow the Lord while they can steal from the bag, and like that *"son of perdition"* (John 17:12), they will sell Him when the thirty pieces of silver are the reward of treachery. Let them know that such gain will involve their souls' eternal loss.

I will apply the words of our text to those who really and spiritually seek Jesus, seek Him as Jesus—the Savior who saves His people from their sins. Such people may be only babes in grace, if indeed they are babes at all. Or they even may be those who cannot say, *"We have found him"* (John 1:45) but who are earnestly *"seeking for Jesus."*

## THE CHARACTER OF SEEKING

In this state of *"seeking for Jesus,"* there is a mingling of good and evil. We see in it much that is of the light, but too much that is of the darkness. It is neither day nor night, a dim twilight, hopeful but clouded over. I might call it "not light, but darkness visible." It is one of those miry places, a marsh, not altogether sea, and certainly not land—like the brackish water of the river's mouth, not altogether salt, but assuredly not sweet.

### Hopefulness in Seeking

*"Seeking for Jesus"* is like an almond tree in blossom; it looks beautiful and has promise, though as yet there is no fruit. The seeker at any rate is not indifferent now. He is not a careless sluggard, demanding yet more sleep and *"folding of the hands"* (Prov. 6:10). He is not a defiant rebel, daring the wrath of God with blasphemous audacity. He is no longer a denier of revelation. He would not be seeking Jesus unless he had some kind of faith—at any rate, a theoretical faith—in a Savior, and in his need of Him.

Now, it is a very encouraging sign when I see men interested and willing to hear. When I can bring men to think, I am very grateful, for thoughtfulness lies on the road to conviction of sin, and conviction is on the way to faith in the Lord Jesus Christ. I am glad, my dear friend, that you are now no longer deaf to the appeals of God's Word. It is well that your ear is open, and even though as yet what you hear is far from bringing you any comfort, rest assured it is a great blessing to you to hear the truth, even when it condemns you. I rejoice to think that you are under concern, and I hope that something may come of it.

Your face is now turned in the right direction, now that you are *"seeking for Jesus."* When you sought sinful pleasure, you were facing the pit of hell; now your face is heavenward. I am glad that Jesus is the object of your search, for depend upon it, nothing else is worth seeking. Salvation from sin and hell should be the first object of your soul's desire. If an alarmed and awakened sinner seeks rest in ceremonies, it will be a search for bread among ashes. If you work for salvation by your own righteousness, you will be looking for substance among dreams. The fact that you are seeking after Jesus shows that you are on the right track, and though as yet you have not reached the haven, the helm is set in the right direction. I am grateful to God for it and encouraged concerning you.

I regard your present state as the little cloud that predicts the coming rain, but I am sorry to say I may be disappointed, and the early cloud may melt into nothingness. Hope tells a flattering tale, but she may be deceived. What a pleasing thing it is to know that a man who has formerly been prayerless is casting himself upon his knees in secret! How gratifying to see the unread Bible brought out from the dust and carefully studied! I think an angel must look on with holy interest when he sees the fresh tear fall in the solitary room and the unaccustomed suppliant bow before his God. Glad are those blessed spirits when they hear the seeker say, "O God, I will seek You until I find You. I will cry to You until I receive an answer of peace." Knowledge of such a vow would make a church rejoice in hope, trusting that the time for newborn children of God to be found in her midst had fully come. A heart that turns itself to Christ, if by chance it may find Him, is evidently in a hopeful condition.

### Doubtfulness in Seeking

The one who seeks after Christ remains disobedient to the great command of the Gospel. If he were obedient to the great gospel precept, he would at once cease to be a seeker and become a happy finder. What is the command of the Gospel? *"Believe on the Lord Jesus Christ, and thou shalt be saved"* (Acts 16:31). Properly speaking, Christ is not an object for seeking; He is not far from any of us. Like the bronze serpent uplifted by Moses, He is not so much to be looked for as looked at. We neither have to clamber to heaven to find Him in the loftiness of His deity and bring Him down, nor dive into the chambers of hades to bring Him up again from the dead. The Lord says,

> *The word is nigh thee, even in thy mouth, and in thy heart: that is, the word of faith, which we preach; that if thou shalt confess with thy mouth the Lord Jesus, and shalt believe in*

> *thine heart that God hath raised him from the*
> *dead, thou shalt be saved.*     *(Rom. 10:8–9)*

Jesus is Immanuel, "God with us." A prayer will reach Him; a wish will find Him; a groan will pierce His heart. You only have to trust in Him, and He is yours. The first command of the Gospel to guilty sinners is not to pray, to search the Scriptures, or to listen to sermons. All these are natural duties, and the man who neglects any of them will come to grief. But the command, the special command, of the Gospel is, *"Believe on the Lord Jesus Christ!"*

Now, the seeking sinner is disobedient to the command. He is going about seeking here and there, but he declines trusting. He is eagerly looking abroad for that which is at home. He is seeking peace far away when it is near to him. He looks east and west to behold a wonder, while the Wonderful, the Savior, stands at his right hand, ready to forgive.

The way of salvation for me as a sinner is simply this: that I, being a sinner, now put my trust in Christ Jesus as the substitute for sinners. God has set forth His crucified Son as the accepted atoning sacrifice for sin. The way of salvation is that I accept Him for the purpose God has set Him forth, namely, as the atonement for my sin, in which I place my sole reliance. Since He is God, since He took upon Himself the nature of man, since as mediator, He suffered in the place of all who trust in Him, I trust Him, and I obtain thereby the blessed result of His sufferings. I am, in fact, thereby saved.

Now, it is certainly a good thing, to some degree, to be a seeker, but it is also a bad thing if I follow my own seeking and refuse God's way of salvation. Hear what the apostle John says: *"He that believeth not God hath made him a liar; because he believeth not the record that God gave of his Son"* (1 John 5:10). This is no small sin to be guilty of, and it entails no small punishment, for *"he that believeth not is condemned already, because he hath not believed in the name of the only begotten Son of God"* (John 3:18).

Suppose that I have a disease and that I have been told of a remedy it. Well, so far it is good that I desire to be cured of my deadly malady; so far it is a hopeful thing that I have sent for a physician. But after being informed that there is one specific remedy for my disease, and that it alone will certainly heal me, if I were still to continue seeking a remedy or to say I am seeking this one true remedy, I would remain sick and ultimately die. I would never be healed unless I took what was prescribed. To seek it is not enough; I must actually take it.

In seeking, then, there is some good, but, oh, how much evil there is also! Here are gleams and flashes of light, but, oh, how dense is the darkness! Here is a little smoke, but I can scarcely call it a spark. Oh, seeker of Jesus, think of this, for while I would not discourage you, I would encourage you to end your seeking by becoming a believer. Do not look at salvation's cup, but drink of it. Do not stand by the edge of the fountain, but wash in it and be clean. Oh, may the Holy Spirit lead you to cease your search for beautiful pearls, for the pearl of great price is before you (Matt. 13:45–46). Jesus is not to be discovered as a secret; He stands before you openly. See His hands and His feet; note well His torn side. And as you look, trust, and from that time He is all your own.

Understand, dear friend, your true position. It is like a soldier on the battlefield, wounded, bleeding, his life slipping away from him. He is perishing, but he is sufficiently aware to know it and to call for help. The surgeon is on the field within hearing; the sufferer pleads for relief with many cries and pleas for help. So far, this is going well, but I implore you to remember that crying out and weeping will not, in and of themselves, heal the sick man. The surgeon must actually come and bind up his wounds. If he refuses to receive the surgeon, he may cry out as much as he wants, but he will bleed to death. So remember that your prayers and seeking, in themselves, cannot save you. Jesus must come to you, and it is madness on your part to refuse Him by your unbelief.

To give another analogy: you are like the murderer of Old Testament times. You have done the murderous deed, and vengeance is armed against you. Swift as lightning, judgment pursues you. You are not now slumbering in foolish security or presumptuously defying the avenger, but, thankfully, you are so aroused that you are running towards the *"city of refuge"* (Josh. 21:13). I delight to think of your earnest running, but run as you may, you are not safe until you are within the city gate. The most vigorous running will not save you if it does not end within the walls of refuge. To enter that open gate, to dwell within that sheltering wall, to enjoy the privilege of sanctuary—this is safety. All else is only hope of escape and not deliverance itself.

To pray, to hear, to desire, to seek—all this is the roadway and the running. But Christ Himself must be laid hold of by faith, or we are not saved.

Run, but take care that you run in God's way, by faith in Jesus and not by trusting in your resolves and feelings. Christ must be yours by personal faith, or you must die eternally.

Let me give yet another picture. You are like one who has been asleep in a burning house. At last you are awakened. The cries of those who would gladly save you have broken your deadly slumbers. You jump up in horror. I think I see you now at the upper window, with the flames drawing near to you. You clearly perceive your danger; you passionately clamor for aid; all your energies are aroused. So far, so good, but all this will not rescue you. You must go to the fire escape, which has now been lifted up to the window. Are you unwilling to take the one and only way of escape? It is close to you; it is suitable; it is efficient; why seek another? There it is, and it is precisely what you need. Your present alarm will only be the prelude of your despair, if you reject the way of escape.

I put these illustrations before you so that you may see that while you are only seeking Jesus, your best friends do not dare to completely hope for you, but are led to tremble, too. We wonder which way the scale will turn. Your future wavers in the balance. As anxious eyes watch a struggling ship making its way with difficulty for port, in imminent danger of the rocks, so we watch you. We see you like Lot and his family, ready to leave Sodom, the city of destruction, but you have not yet reached the mountain. Our hearts ask, concerning you, "Will he linger in the plain? Will he look back? Or will he be delivered completely?" If you remain as you are, there is no hope for you. All the supposed good that is now in you is vanity itself if it leaves you short of Christ. Remember this verse well:

> Why those fears, poor seeking sinner?
>    Why those anxious, gloomy fears?
> Sighs and sorrowings cannot save thee,
>    Healing dwells not in thy tears;
>       'Tis believing
>    Which the soul to Christ endears.

## THE PERPLEXITIES OF SEEKING

### Ignorance

*"Seeking for Jesus"* is a state of heart in which the poor soul is usually very distressed. He is "tumbled up and down in his thoughts," as John Bunyan would say, for seekers are initially very often greatly perplexed as the result of their ignorance of the way of salvation. Too often, awakened souls, though they may have heard the Gospel, do not understand it in their hearts. Many inquirers do not know what faith is. I am persuaded that millions do not know what believing in Jesus means. Though they are told every Sunday, they cannot grasp the concept, for the Spirit of God has not illuminated their minds.

To believe in Jesus, as I say again and again and again, is simply to trust in Jesus—to take God at His word, to take Christ for what God says He is, namely, the Atonement, the satisfaction for sin, the Savior of sinners. But poor, troubled consciences think faith is a deep mystery, and they go about like blind men groping for the wall. They wander like travelers in a dense fog, not knowing which way leads to their homes, hoping, but hoping against hope by reason of ignorance. Many, though they desire to be saved, do not understand the work of Christ or know what atonement is.

Though the doctrine of substitution, which is the very marrow of the Gospel, is so very plain to believers, many seekers have not learned it. That Jesus bore the sin of His people; that *"the LORD hath laid on him the iniquity of us all"* (Isa. 53:6); that He was made sin for us; that justice received its due at His hands—many penitent sinners have not grasped this precious fact. They still think there is so much repentance to do, so much feeling to endure, so much praying to go through, so much mystery to be experienced. But the plain, simple precept, "Believe and live," trust and be accepted, hide under the shadow of the cross and be safe—this, through ignorance, they do not understand. This involves them in trouble upon trouble until their way is hedged up with thorns.

### Fear

At such times, too, to increase their perplexity, they are usually distracted with fear. People in a panic act generally in the worst conceivable manner for their own safety, and an awakened sinner is in much the same condition. A terrible sound is in his ears. He hears the rumbling of the everlasting tempest; he sees the gathering storm. He does not know what to do or where to flee. His sins, which once appeared as such trifles, now rise before him like mountains of blackness. The wrath of God, which at one time he defied, makes him fear and tremble exceedingly. He sees the dark record of his transgressions and anticipates the hour when all his sins will be read before the assembled universe, and the sentence of wrath will go forth against him. Where will he flee? He scarcely knows how or where to fly.

A spirit distracted with dread is never a wise spirit and often is goaded on to madness. Pressed beyond measure with apprehension in his heart and warnings from his conscience, many a man who has refused to believe in Jesus has done violence to himself. Do you wonder, then, that souls under a sense of sin and fear of wrath are far from being calm and collected, but rather are like mariners in a storm, who *"reel to and fro, and stagger like a drunken man"* (Ps. 107:27)? How soon would their bewilderment end in sweet rest if they would obey the divine mandate and accept the great salvation!

### A Thousand Questions

The newly-awakened mind is very apt to lose itself in the many spiritual problems that lie before it. The man cared nothing for these matters before, but now he has even a morbid craving after knowledge. He seems as if he could not learn too much or too fast. How many inquirers, instead of turning to the Cross, worry themselves with intricacies of doctrine, debatable points that belong rather to metaphysics than to divinity! They are fascinated by the *"things hard to be understood"* (2 Pet. 3:16) and forget the truths that a wondering man, though a fool, may readily comprehend.

How many ask themselves, "Are we elect?" when their inquiry should be, "How can a man be cleansed from iniquity?" Indeed, they must learn Latin and Greek before they know their alphabet and must fathom the doctrine of election before they will believe in the redemption of Jesus. They would come to the Father before they have come to the Son and learn their predestination before their pardon. They attempt to grapple with that which has perplexed the wisest of men, namely, how to reconcile divine ordination with the free will of man, while they are in danger of the unquenchable fire. They philosophize at hell's mouth and debate in the jaws of perdition.

You may show them how absurd it is, as absurd as it is for a drowning man to wish to quibble about hydraulics and refuse to lay hold of the friendly rope until he understands some mystery in hydrostatics. Or, it is as absurd as if an extremely sick person refused all surgery until he understood anatomy and comprehended the secret influences of drugs upon the different portions of the body. Yet some inquirers will remain in this folly. I do not wonder at it, when I remember how foolish man is by nature. Men who have left the whole spiritual realm untrodden are very apt, when they see it open up suddenly before their eyes, to aspire in their hearts' pride to stand upon its loftiest peaks, to climb its Himalayas, to swim its English Channel, to fathom its Atlantic, and for this reason they forget its green pastures and still waters.

I want every convinced sinner to pay attention to what I am saying. Friends, sinners such as you are, you have to deal with the plain truth of the Gospel—namely this: *"Christ Jesus came into the*

*world to save sinners"* (1 Tim. 1:15). Faith links you
to that Savior. When you have learned that lesson,
then you will discover that God has chosen you from
the beginning, that He has ordained you for eternal
life. But, as yet, you cannot decipher that matter.
Leave that glorious doctrine until your soul is saved
by faith in Jesus Christ. It is plain, however, that
this appetite for strong meat takes the babe away
from the pure milk of the Word. These questions
help to confuse, trouble, worry, and distract the
seeker of Jesus.

At this hour, too, to make confusion more con-
founded, Satan is quite sure to assail the soul with
his diabolical insinuations and suggestions, with
strong temptations and despairing thoughts. No
king will willingly lose his subjects, and Satan, when
he sees his captives about to turn away, sets extra
guards around them. He will set others on to tempt
them, or he will come himself personally and inject
into the soul the most horrible thoughts, the most
blasphemous suggestions, and the most despairing
forebodings that can be conceived of.

Having experienced these things, I speak ten-
derly to those who may now be bothered by them.
Do not marvel at them or be dismayed. If you can, by
the Holy Spirit's help, resist Satan; he will flee from
you. If you can assail him with *"It is written"* (Matt.
4:4), he will leave you, but do not be astonished if
now for awhile the fiery darts fly as thick as hail. He
has his machine guns from which he can vomit ten
thousand shots at once upon a poor lost soul and
make it feel as though it were broken in pieces with
horror and dismay. You will triumph over him yet if
you believe. The Lord will bruise Satan under your

feet shortly. Be of good courage! Though you fall, you will rise again; faith will lift you up in the power of Jesus. I do not marvel that when that dog of hell howls in your ears, it is painfully difficult for your spirit to find comfort.

## Not Ceasing from Sin

It may be also that when the soul is seeking Jesus, it is at the same time much grieved to find it cannot even now cease from sin. "I want to be rid of my old sins," says the heart, "but how can I hope for forgiveness, for I have sinned this very day? I went to my room, and I bowed my knee and said, *'God be merciful to me a sinner'* (Luke 18:13). I came downstairs resolved to be watchful, but something annoyed me, and I spoke unadvisedly. How can I think God will have mercy on me?" Or says another, "I was seeking the Savior this morning, but I went out to my business and I met with worldly company, and I forgot my Lord. I am afraid I mingled with them so closely that I participated in their sinful behavior, and now how can the Lord have any pity upon such a hypocritical seeker as I have been?" As if that poor heart expected to be perfect before it had even found pardon! As if a patient expected to be perfectly well before he had followed the advice of his physician!

My dear reader, if you were able to cease from all sin for a single day, I am sure you would be out of place on earth, for heaven is the place for perfect people, not this sinful earth. If a fountain sent forth nothing but pure water for one whole day, we might conclude that it was completely purified. The bearing of good fruit for one season would prove that a tree was good. If your heart abstained from sin by itself throughout one day, it might for another, and so on, forever, and then what would be the need of a Savior? What, do you not know that Christ came to save you from your new sins as well as from your old transgressions? Is His arm too short to reach your daily needs? Is His blood of too little power to wash away your fresh pollutants? Do you still have some hope of bettering yourself?

Be done with this trifling. Confess that you are a helpless sinner, shaped in iniquity, conceived in sin, depraved in heart, and, therefore, needing the never-ceasing mercy of the Lord your God. Come, wash now in the fountain filled with blood, and if sin returns, ask Jesus to wash your feet again. Make Jesus your sole reliance. Cry to Him, *"Purge me with hyssop, and I shall be clean: wash me, and I shall be whiter than snow"* (Ps. 51:7). Nothing else can end your perplexities; you cannot untie the Gordian knot of your difficulties. Cut it, then, by leaving all to Jesus. You cannot overcome your sins except by the blood of the Lamb. You cannot be what you should be or what you want to be except by taking Jesus to be your all in all. Here is a song for you:

> At last I own it cannot be
> That I should fit myself for thee:
> Here, then, to thee I all resign;
> Thine is the work, and only thine.
>
> What shall I say thy grace to move?
> I give up every plea beside,
> Lord, I am sin, but thou art love:
> Lord, I am lost—but thou hast died!

## THE DANGERS OF SEEKING

I have already told you that there is much that is hopeful in your condition, but, that there is also much danger in it.

### Wasting Time and Losing Comfort

This long-continued seeking is a sad thing, when it might all end so happily even now at this present hour. If you had believed in Jesus at the very first, you would have had light at once. How often would He have gathered you, as a hen gathers her chickens under her wings, but you would not come! If you will trust Him now, the daystar will shine in your heart.

You are like Hopeful and Christian in Giant Despair's castle, as told by John Bunyan in *The Pilgrim's Progress*. They lamented and bemoaned their common sorrow and planned diverse, unavailable methods of escape, but, at last, Christian, as someone half amazed, broke out into this passionate speech: "What a fool am I," says he, "to lie in this stinking dungeon, when I may as well walk at liberty! I have a key in my bosom called Promise, that will, I am persuaded, open any lock in Doubting Castle." Then Hopeful said, "that's good news, good brother. Pluck it out of your bosom, and try."

My awakened reader, this is your condition. You have in your heart, and you have in God's Word, that which will unlock every door in your prison house. Get up, and try it now. Can you not believe that Jesus is the Christ, and that God has sent Jesus to bear your sin? Can you not trust in Him? If you can, you are free. Your sins are forgiven, and you are saved.

## "Seeking for Jesus"

You have perhaps heard of the incident of a dove
pursued by a hawk. The frightened bird flew into the
chest of a man who was walking in the fields, and
you remember that it was safely protected by him
whom it had trusted. The dove would not of itself
have flown there, but under the terror of the hawk it
sought a shelter. You have been afraid of Jesus; you
have thought He would not receive you. But now
that hell pursues you, be venturesome, and fly to
Him. Say as this hymn puts it:

> I can but perish if I go;
> I am resolved to try;
> For if I stay away, I know
> I must forever die.

If Christ stood with a drawn sword in His hand,
you had better run on the point of His sword than
perish without Him. Oh, come to Him, driven by
desperation itself, if by nothing else; come into His
embrace! You will have peace at once. But all the
while you remain seeking, I do not know in what distracted manner, you are wasting time. You are
missing comfort, and you are losing opportunities for
happiness. Cease your seeking, for there is the Man
whom you seek. He stands revealed before you.
Reach out your finger and put it into the mark of the
nails, or if that is too bold, touch the hem of His
garment, and you will be made whole.

### Being Driven to Despair

I do not doubt that some people who were once
sincere but unrenewed seekers have now given up all

thought of seeking Christ because they continued to seek when He was near them, to look for Him instead of looking to Him. They have waited so long in prayer and Bible reading, and so on, that now they utterly despair and give up all as hopeless. It is no wonder. If you try to do a thing in a wrong way, you cannot hope to succeed. If a man will not plow and sow, he will not reap. If you will not believe, you will not be established.

A person may be very industrious indeed in what he does, but if he follows a method that can never produce the result he desires, he must not be surprised when he is disappointed. You are a seeker, and I am glad you are, but if you will not put your trust in Jesus and lay your burden down at the cross where He offered the great sacrifice, it is no marvel if you continue to seek in vain. It will be a great sorrow, but it will not be a great wonder, if you finally become despairing and are shut up in the iron cage. Oh, break away from this. May God's Holy Spirit come to your rescue now! Give up your own ideas of how to get peace, take God's method of salvation, and lay hold of eternal life by trusting in the slain Savior.

### Seeking Can Die Out in Indifference

Having sought by prayer and failing to find peace at once, temptations to go back to the world's pleasure attack the soul, and too often it becomes henceforth impervious to exhortations and objections. The unbroken, unrenewed heart grows sullen and declares, "I tried, but I did not succeed. I may as well have what pleasure I can have, for spiritual joys are denied me. If the world to come cannot be mine,

I will have this world and take my fill of it." I pray you may never be driven to that, but my fear is that if you wait long in this borderland, seeking but yet halting between two opinions, undecided and unbelieving, you will finally relapse into your former state of spiritual slumber. Then your last end will be worse than the first (2 Pet. 2:20).

## Taking Up with Something Short of Jesus

I have known people who have been content to remain seekers all their days. They have felt comforted by the thought that they are seekers. Now, such comfort is like plastering with unmixed mortar.

Imagine an unemployed man who has been walking up and down the London streets to find something to do. His family is in need, and he must find a job. He is quite right to seek, but he will not be satisfied with seeking; he wants to find. Tramping the street will not feed his children. He is not content with having called at many shops. He will not rest until he finds what he is after, and he would be very foolish if he did. So, to be a seeker of Christ, walking up and down the streets, as it were, will not fill your hungry soul. You must get Christ Himself.

If any unemployed father of a family were to say, "Well, I walk about so many days in the week, and so many hours in the day, and I am quite satisfied, though I do not find anything to do," you would think he was a great fool. And so it is with you. It is a good sign when there is an appetite, but a mere appetite does not satisfy a man. He must eat the food provided. Seeking Christ will not save you, unless it leads you truly to believe in Jesus.

It is a bad sign when a man says, "Well, I am doing my best. I am always at a place of worship. I am a Bible reader. I practice prayer at home. I do my best." My dear friend, if you settle down in that idea, you are self-righteous and are off the road altogether. Besides, you are lying to your own heart, for, after all, you are at enmity with God, and the sign of that enmity is this: that you refuse to believe in His dear Son. If you were reconciled to God, you would love Jesus Christ and trust in Him. I see what it is: you have resolved, after all, to be your own savior. You still think that there is something in outward religion that will produce salvation, whereas, I solemnly assure you that, if you stubbornly resist believing in Christ, if you will not fly to those dear wounds of His, if you will not hide beneath the shelter of the Atonement, you will go to hell just as well from a place of worship as from the haunts of sin, and will perish as certainly with a Bible read as with a Bible burned.

> None but Jesus, none but Jesus,
> Can do helpless sinners good.

"Oh, but," you say, "I feel my sins so much!" Yes, but if you trust in your feelings, you will perish in them as much as though you wallowed in your sins. Oh, soul, resolve with Toplady:

> He that suffer'd in my stead,
>     Shall my Physician be;
> I will not be comforted
>     Till Jesus comforts me.

Never hope to be saved except by God's way of salvation. Oh, that the Holy Spirit would enable you in your heart to say, "Now I come to You, Jesus. Guilty as I am, I lift my eyes to You, and this is my prayer: 'Help me for Your mercy's sake. Have pity on me, and cleanse me in Your blood, for I put all my trust in You.'" Resolve, to have no refuge of lies, no Savior but the Lamb of God.

I will confess to you, dear seeker, that often I am myself personally driven to do what I believe you may be led to do today. I look back upon my past life, and while I have much to thank God for, much in which I can see His Spirit's hand, when I feel my responsibilities and my shortcomings, my heart sinks within me. I think of my transgressions, better known to myself than to anyone else, and I remember too that they are not known even to me as they are to God. Then I feel all hope swept away and my soul left in utter despair until I come anew to the cross and think of who it was who died there and why He died and what purposes of infinite mercy are fulfilled by His death.

It is so sweet to look up to the Crucified One again and say, "I have nothing but You, my Lord, no confidence but You. If You are not accepted as my substitute, I must perish. If God's appointed Savior is not enough, I have no other. But I know You are the Father's Well Beloved, and I am accepted in You. You are all I want and all I have." How I desire, with intense longing, that you may do the same. It would be a blessed day for you and a joyful occasion for me. The Jews, in the chapter from which our text comes, asked our Savior, *"What shall we do, that we might work the works of God?"* (John 6:28), and He said, *"This is the work of God, that ye believe on him whom he hath sent"* (v. 29). The greatest of all works, the most godlike work, is to stop self-righteous seeking and trust in Jesus.

## DIRECTIONS TO THOSE WHO ARE SEEKING

### Give Attention to the Object of Faith

The only way by which you can be saved is by faith. Understand that to be settled fact. Now, if a man says, "I cannot believe such a thing," what then? What is his wisest course? Suppose you find it difficult to believe some report. What do you do? Why, you consider the probabilities of it.

Suppose it is rumored that the Emperor Napoleon had shot himself. Will I believe the report? I will ask where the rumor comes from, what intelligence corroborates it, upon what authority it is stated, and so on. By that means I will arrive at a conclusion that either it is probably true or is only a frivolous tale.

Now, if you earnestly desire to believe, faith is the gift of God and a work of the Spirit. But God works according to the laws of mind, and faith in Christ will most readily come to you in conformity with those laws.

*"Faith cometh by hearing"* (Rom. 10:17). How does it come by hearing? Why, because by hearing I learn the truth concerning Christ. What I hear commends itself to my judgment and understanding, and so I come to believe. Faith comes to us by reading, which is another form of hearing. Read what the Scripture has to say about the Messiah and His work, and you will be helped to believe God's testimony by knowing what it is and on what authority it

comes to you. Let your hearing and your reading be accompanied with meditation. Like the Virgin Mary, ponder these things in your heart. *"Incline your ear,"* says the Spirit, *"and come unto me: hear, and your soul shall live"* (Isa. 55:3).

Now, inclining your ear means a devout and diligent attention to the Good News and a weighing of it in your inmost heart. Now look at it. You have sinned, and God must punish sin. These two facts are clear enough to your conscience. Is it not a marvelous system that God should be pleased to put away sin through an atonement by laying the sin upon another and punishing it in the person of His Son? Do you know of any other system that would satisfy the case so well, that would be so suitable to you? I believe that the authenticity of Scripture is better proved by the very existence of this doctrine than by anything else, for no human mind could ever have contrived or conceived of a way so just to God and yet so infinitely gracious. I feel sure it is true; I am certain of it.

Then, I find it promised over and over again by God Himself that if I trust Christ I will have the benefit of all His work. I therefore believe the thing is reasonable; it is proclaimed by divine authority. I have God's promise for it. I know that the Almighty One cannot lie. I cheerfully accept what He provides for me, and I am saved.

My dear reader, if you find it hard to believe, shut yourself in you room today, and do not come out again until you have pictured in your mind's eye the everlasting God setting aside His indescribable splendors and taking upon Himself the nature of man. Imagine that glorious One nailed to Calvary's tree, forsaken by God, crying out in anguish, and dying without a friend—all to make an atonement to the law of God! As You are fixing your eyes upon this and bowing in humble prayer, faith will come to you. The Holy Spirit will overshadow you, and it will be conceived in your soul. Faith will drop in your soul like the dew from heaven. You will be amazed to find that the hardness of your heart is all gone and that your unbelief has all departed, and you will say, *"Lord, I believe; help thou mine unbelief"* (Mark 9:24).

### Stay Away from Whatever Will Hinder Belief

Now, you may depend upon the fact that going into sin hinders believing. You cannot continue in willful sin and yet become a believer. Sin cherished in the heart is an effective hindrance. A man cannot be tied to a post and yet run away at the same time. If you bind yourself to your sin, you cannot escape. Withdraw at once from evil company—it brings a very deadly injury to young seekers. You hear an impressive sermon, but when you go away and talk with idle gossips and fall into frivolous chitchat, you cannot expect your soul to grow in the right direction under such influences. Get on your knees, go into solitude, go to your God, go to Jesus Christ. This is what will roll away the stone that blocks the door.

And, once again, remember that until you have believed, your danger is of the most imminent kind. You are not in danger of something only in the future. You are in peril even now, for the wrath of God remains on you. You are not like a city that is to be attacked by troops that are at a distance; the Judge is even now at the door. You are actually being besieged. The foes have encompassed you. They are lifting the scaling ladders, and they will soon scale the walls. Beware, sinner, beware, for your present state is terrible. Your future state will be hopeless. Today is the accepted time. It is now or never with some of you. Escape now for your lives. Seek now, but seek in the right way: by believing in Him who is the Savior of the sons of men.

How I have longed to tell you these things in passionate earnestness, for I hunger for your salvation. This comes from my soul, but I cannot tell it as I would like to or else I would saturate these pages with my tears. Oh, that the Master might bless even my weakness by carrying home the truth to your hearts and consciences. I do not like the idea of anyone reading these words without thinking these things over and giving his or her heart to Jesus. I tell you these things in God's name. Oh, now, before you have put this book down, let me implore you one more time with this Scripture passage: *"Look unto me, and be ye saved, all the ends of the earth"* (Isa. 45:22). It is the cry of the crucified Savior. Do not turn away from that dear voice that is so full of anguish. Do not hide your eyes from that brow still marked with the crown of thorns. Do not despise those nailed hands and feet, but yield to Him as again He cries in agony, out of His deep love of us, *"Look unto me, and be ye saved, all the ends of the earth."* O Lord, do turn them, and they will be turned.

## Chapter 4

# The Joy of Finding God

*"They shall praise the LORD that seek him."*
—Psalm 22:26

The words of Jesus on the cross, *"My God, my God, why hast thou forsaken me?"* (Ps. 22:1) were written by the inspired prophet just before the words of our text. When the Savior uttered these words, He may have implied the entire psalm from which they came, including verse twenty-six. On the cross, He had just passed through the experience of a seeker, as far as it was possible for Him to do so. He had been engaged in earnest, fervent, pleading prayer, because He had been left without His Father's presence. He had had the following words in mind, *"Be not thou far from me, O LORD: O my strength, haste thee to help me"* (v. 19). With strong crying and tears He had pleaded for salvation from the lion's mouth. He had at last been heard and delivered, and He exclaimed with joy:

*He hath not despised nor abhorred the affliction of the afflicted; neither hath he hid his face from him; but when he cried unto him, he*

> *heard. My praise shall be of thee in the great*
> *congregation: I will pay my vows before them*
> *that fear him.* (Ps. 22:24–25)

Thus, you see, because He had known the agony of an anxious seeker, He had been heard in His seeking, and therefore He felt praise rising in His own soul. He learned sympathy with all seeking souls of every age and foresaw that they also would magnify the name of the Lord. Jesus knows every experience, for He has passed through the same.

Does this thought not already whisper comfort to your soul? My seeking friend, is it not a good sign that Jesus was heard saying that He feared? Does the fact that Jesus can sympathize with you not raise some hope in your heart? It is true He never lived without the presence of God, as you have done, in consequence of personal sin. But, He was forsaken by God for a magnificent reason, namely, because He stood in our place, and therefore was compelled to cry to Him, even as you are doing, *"My God, my God, why hast thou forsaken me? why art thou so far from helping me?"* (v. 1). Therefore, He understands the grief that troubles your fainting heart. He understands all your distresses while you are fretting and lamenting that you cry in the daytime and the Lord does not hear, and that in the night you plead in vain (v. 2). This reflection at the outset of our discussion should be like the note of a silver bell: soft, and restful to your weary ear. Jesus foretells your success in seeking, as the result of His own experience.

Our Lord's great purpose in laying down His life on the cross was the Father's glory. No other purpose was worthy of Him. He sought the salvation of

men to the glory of God, and so, in His extreme agonies, our Lord Jesus placed this joy before Himself
and consoled Himself by foreseeing that God would
be praised by souls who would seek Him as a result
of His death. He comforted Himself with the reflection, *"All the ends of the world shall remember and
turn unto the LORD: and all the kindreds of the nations shall worship before thee"* (v. 27). He dwelled
on the truth that *"they shall praise the LORD that
seek him,"* and He saw in this honoring of God the
reward that His soul sought.

What He foresaw from His lookout upon the
cross is actually taking place every day, for seekers
are learning to be singers. How will the choirs of
heaven be filled? As yet there are many vacant seats,
and the full chorus has not yet been heard. From
where will they who will complete that orchestra
come? They will be called by grace from among ungodly men and be led to long for God: *"They shall
praise the LORD that seek him."* Fear not, for the
number of the elect will be accomplished, and no
part of heaven's music will flag for lack of musicians.
From the choirs of earth, devout believers are being
withdrawn, one by one, to unite in the harmonies of
heaven. Just when their voices become most mellow
and most clear, they leave us for the ivory palaces
and their ceaseless melodies.

How will the praises of God be maintained here
below? If, one by one, the sweet voices grow silent,
and the singers are laid in the sepulcher, from where
will we replenish our numbers and maintain the
daily praise? Fear not, there are new voices on the
way. *"They shall praise the LORD that seek him."*
There are souls who are now weeping for sin and

85

longing for a Savior, who will soon find Him, and they will then become very hearty singers of the new song. They are coming, coming in their thousands even now. The music of praise will be continued as long as the sun shines, and the glory of the Lord will cover the earth as the waters cover the sea (Hab. 2:14). From generation to generation, the name of the Lord will be praised.

This brings great gladness to my spirit, for I know that there are some who are seeking the Savior, and I rejoice to know that they will soon be among the most earnest in praising the name of the Lord. They will not always wear sackcloth; they will put on the silken garments of praise before long. There are some who are secretly searching for my Lord. The Lord has seen them as He saw Nathanael under the fig tree.

There are young children seeking. Boys and girls who do not yet dare to speak to their parents are praying for grace in private. Blessed be the Savior of the young. These little ones will grow up and praise God when their fathers have gone to their reward. Young men and women, too, are turning to Christ, though perhaps they would blush if they were personally charged with the holy search. Men, too, who are in their prime are coming to Jesus to spend their strength in the service of the Redeemer.

The Lord is gently touching many hearts and drawing them to Himself, and each one, when he finds the Lord, will make a sweet singer to swell the tune of divine grace. Perhaps there may even be some aged people reading this book whose voices are becoming feeble as the years go by. Nevertheless, they will sing with their hearts most melodiously to the glory of the God of all long-suffering. Whoever they are, when they have found the Lord Jesus Christ, they must and will glorify the God of their salvation. So you see the great purpose of our Lord Jesus was that God might be praised, and He knew beforehand that this purpose would be effected by the praises of those who, in seeking, would find His grace.

This assurance that Christ gives, that *"they shall praise the LORD that seek him,"* ought to be very encouraging to all seekers, for, my dear friends, it is wise for you to seek the Lord even if you had no stronger hope than a mere, *"peradventure he will save* [us]" (1 Kings 20:31). It would be wise to do as the men of Nineveh did, to repent and turn to God, even if you had nothing better than *"Who can tell?"* (Jonah 3:9) to encourage you in so doing. But since our Lord Jesus Christ, in dying, felt confident that seekers would find peace and joy, and so would come to praise God, we have double comfort. He could not have been mistaken, rest assured of that; therefore, seekers will have reasons for praising the Lord.

It is from the fact that He died upon the cross that it becomes certain that the seeker will be a finder. This was what made Him sustain the scorn of men, the faintness of fever, the darkness of death, and the horror of desertion. He knew that His agonizing humility on the cross and His yielding up of His spirit would render it certain that no seeking soul would ever seek the Lord in vain. If there had been no suffering Savior, there would have been no way to God. If there had been no dying Christ, there would have been no living consolation. But, now that His atoning work has been accomplished, and He has said, *"It is finished"* (John 19:30), they who seek Him will live, and their lives will be spent praising Him.

Now, there are three things that our text, *"They shall praise the LORD that seek him,"* is concerned with: the people, the promise, and the praise.

## THE PEOPLE

Notice how unrestricted the description of the people is: *"They shall praise the LORD that seek him."* It does not say that only certain people who seek God will praise Him, but that anyone who seeks Him will ultimately praise Him. You, my dear reader, are included among the rest. None are excluded from the sweep of this precious promise, provided they are really seekers. In other matters, many seek and only a few find, but the rule of the gospel kingdom is *"he that seeketh findeth"* (Matt. 7:8). This rule has no exceptions.

But what is meant by "seeking" the Lord? Who are the true seekers to whom this promise is made?

### Those Who Desire to Commune with God

Some are satisfied with the mere form when they say a prayer, but he who really prays desires to converse with God. He longs for his desires to be heard by the Most High and to obtain the needed blessings for which he asks. No devotion can ever satisfy a true heart but that which brings him into contact with the Most High. We do not seek fine words in prayer; we do not seek choice music in praise; we do not seek the church; we seek God.

When any man is really stirred to seek God, although he may not know much yet of the true faith, he has a desire within him to which the Lord always gives an answer of peace. You may be quite ignorant of the doctrine and teaching of the Lord Jesus, but if, in any nation, any man will really seek the only living and true God, he will receive further light and will ultimately come to praise the Lord.

## Those Who Are Conscious of Having Strayed

Those who seek God Himself very soon discover that they are at a distance from Him. A man does not seek what he has, and what is close at hand is not an object of search. But when a man longs for God, there suddenly springs up in his soul a consciousness that he has departed from the Most High. So he cries to the Lord to remove the separating mountains and to fill up the dividing valleys, and he who truly does this is the man who will yet live to praise God.

## Those Who Are Anxious to Remove Obstacles to God

If unpardoned sin has kept one from God, the true seeker longs for such forgiveness as God may justly give. If the obstacle is the power of sin in his members, the earnest seeker cries for power to overcome every thought of evil. The awakened soul soon becomes conscious that nothing separates him from God like the love of sin, and therefore he seeks to have sin slain and lust crucified and the enmity towards God forever destroyed. How we long to be delivered from every false way, from every pollutant, and even from every appearance of evil that would tend to prevent our walking in happy fellowship with God! We know that two cannot walk together unless they are agreed (Amos 3:3). Therefore, seeking the Lord leads the soul to grieve over sin and to strive with all his might with holy violence to break away from harmful habits that bind him and to tread underfoot tendencies that would lead him astray.

Are you conscious, dear friend, of such a seeking of God as this? Do you desire Him as the weary watcher on the castle wall desires the morning light? Do you pray to have everything taken away from you that separates you and your God? Do you long for someone to bridge the chasm and to bring you near to the Lord in spirit and in truth? If such is the case, the promise of the text is certainly yours. *"They shall praise the LORD that seek him."*

### Those Who Long to Be a Friend of God

Oh, the sweetness of knowing that there is nothing between God and you but goodwill and love, that all the sad past is forgiven and even blotted out of the Lord's remembrance, that now you may speak to Him without fear, and that you may trust in Him without dread. Atonement has removed His righteous wrath and securely established His boundless love. Now you may come and lie in His arms, for they are your Father's arms. You may even hide under the dark shadow of His wing, for it is your Father's wing. It will cover you from all harm as a hen covers her chickens. It is the prelude of heaven to know what the following verse describes:

## The Joy of Finding God

The God that rules on high
And thunders when He please,
That rides upon the stormy sky,
And manages the seas,
This awful God is ours.

All His power is for our protection. All His wisdom is for our direction. All His tenderness is for our consolation. All His truth is for our encouragement. All His grandeur is for our ennobling. All the infinity of His nature is for our eternal glorification. He wills that we should be partakers of the divine nature and dwellers in the divine blessedness. This is very precious, and this is what the soul who seeks God is searching for. He aspires to walk with God and to dwell with God. He longs to abide in Him, to be His beloved forever, to be accepted in Christ Jesus, and to become daily more and more conformed to the divine image. Our grand ambition is to be cleansed from everything that is alien to the design and the nature of God and to be perfectly at one with God. Oh, beloved, this is a blessed longing for a soul to have, and he who has it, though he may mourn and sorrow now, will one day praise and bless God.

### Those Who Seek God Now

God hates the idea of postponement. To a seeking soul, a moment's delay is a dreadful thought: he desires immediate salvation and wants to be reconciled to God at once. As the hungry man does not wish the meal to be postponed but would rather be fed immediately, so the true seeker's heart and flesh cry out after God, for the living God. As the deer pants for the water, the seeker's soul pants after God (Ps. 42:1). This desire is continuous and cannot be turned to another object.

A man cannot always perceive this desire with equal vividness because he is in the world and his thoughts must be somewhat diverted by his ordinary business and the cares of it. But still the desire is always alive in his soul, and whenever the stress of worldly care is taken from his mind, his heart flies back to its longings and begins again to sigh and cry after God. Such a man will break away from his companions to plead with God alone. He will be praying without so much as the movement of his lips, even when he is in the company of others. He will lie awake at night tossing on his bed and saying, "Oh, that I knew where I might find Him." He will wake in the morning with this desire strong upon him and will seek the Lord as one who searches for hidden treasure.

This desire hovers over the man who is subject to it, overshadows his being, and masters him completely. I have known it to deprive food of its tastefulness and home of its comfort, and make the seeker cry, "Woe is me until I find my God. I draw near to the gates of death until He appears. Let others ask for the increase of their crops and wine. Lord, lift up the light of Your countenance upon me, for this and this only will content my soul."

Now, beloved, all this seeking by the soul, which I have feebly described, prepares a man for praising God when he finds mercy at the Cross, as you will readily see upon reflection. This is the Holy Spirit's way of tuning the harp for future singing of psalms. No man can praise God like the believer who has sought the Savior, sorrowing as His mother and Joseph did in the days when He was on earth, and at last found Him.

The seeker knows the bitterness of sin, and therefore he can appreciate the sweetness of pardoning mercy. He has been made to know his own lost state, and in consequence he will rejoice all the more when he is found by the Good Shepherd and restored to his home by his Great Father. He knows his helplessness—no one knows it better—for he has tried the works of the law and failed. He has even tried prayer and gospel ordinances, and he has not succeeded in them to the point where he has found rest for his soul in them. He knows that he is broken in pieces, all apart. Therefore, when he who considers himself to be such a helpless worm finds his help in the Lord Jesus, what praises Christ will have and what love He will receive in return for all His gracious aid!

The poor seeker has known in his own heart what he deserves at the hands of the law. He has had a glimpse of the world to come and the terrors of judgment and the burning of eternal wrath, and with the unquenchable fire scorching his very face, he must and will praise his Deliverer who has plucked him as a brand out of the burning. All his seeking, I say, helps him to prize divine mercy when he receives it and trains him to praise God according to the promise of our text, *"They shall praise the LORD that seek him."*

Never is a child as dear to his mother as when he has just been restored from a sickness that threatened his life. Never does a father rejoice over his little child so much as when he has been lost for a long time in the woods and is at last brought home after a weary search. No gold is so precious to a man as that which he has earned by hard labor and self-denial; the harder he has toiled to gain it, the more joyful he is when he finally has enough to permit him to rest. No freedom is as precious as the newly found liberty of a slave, no charitable enlargement of the heart so joyous as that of one who has been sitting in the valley of the shadow of death for a long time, bound in affliction and iron. No return to a country is so full of delight as that of sorrowful exiles who come back from cruel Babylon, by whose waters they sat and wept, yes, wept when they remembered Zion (Ps. 137:1).

> *When the LORD turned again the captivity of Zion, we were like them that dream. Then was our mouth filled with laughter, and our tongue with singing: then said they among the heathen, The LORD hath done great things for them. The LORD hath done great things for us; whereof we are glad.* (Ps. 126:1–3)

If there are any seekers reading this, I hope that if they have seen themselves in the picture that I have outlined, they will be still further enabled to take heart and be of good courage. I am trying hard to drop words of comfort, just as in the story of Ruth, who came into the field of Boaz when the reapers purposefully dropped handfuls of grain for her so that she might glean and return with a full portion.

### THE PROMISE

Our text, *"They shall praise the LORD that seek him,"* is a blessed promise! It is gradually but surely fulfilled.

## The Joy of Finding God

### It Is Fulfilled Unconsciously While One Is Seeking

Did you ever think of this? Without knowing it, the humble seeker is already praising God. That confession of sin, which he made with so many tears, glorified God by bearing witness to the justice of God's law and the truth of the charges that it brings against our fallen nature. *"Joshua said unto Achan, My son, give, I pray thee, glory to the LORD God of Israel, and make confession unto him"* (Josh. 7:19).

There is a measure of true praise in confession, and it is as pure and real as that which angels present before the sapphire throne. When the seeker acknowledges that he deserves to be sent to hell, he is, in fact, praising justice; he is adoring the Judge of all. In so doing he brings a mixture of unbelief and a forgetfulness of God's other attributes. Yet he has a firm belief in divine justice and an entreating adoration of it that is far from being unacceptable.

In the seeker there is also a measure of delight in God's mercy. While the poor sin-stricken soul is craving pardon, he confesses heartily how sweet mercy is in itself if he might only obtain it. He says how gracious forgiveness is, how precious lovingkindness is if he might only be favored with them. No living man has so keen an eye to the tender attributes of God as he whose soul is covered all over with wounds and bruises and decaying sores, through a sense of sin.

The seeking soul is really praising the Lord Jesus by appreciating the preciousness of His love and the value of His blood and saying within himself, "Oh, that I might know the value of these in my own case! Oh, that I could but touch the hem of His garment for myself! If only I knew what it is to be washed in His blood and to be covered with His righteousness!" There is in all these emotions a measure of latent praise nonetheless accepted by the Lord because it is not perceived by man. There is a precious fragrance of deep reverence and holy awe about a seeker's prayers that render them sweet to the Lord. So, you see, the seeker is already praising God and thus in a measure the promise is fulfilled.

### Praise Exceedingly Abounds

As a bird lies hidden among the heather, but is seen when at last it is startled and flies away, praise takes to the wing and displays itself when at last those who seek the Lord are permitted to find Him. What thunderclaps of praise come from poor sinners when they have just found their all in all in God in the person of Christ Jesus! Then their joy becomes almost too much for them to hold, vastly too much for them to express. Oh, the praises, the day and night praises, the continuous praises, that rise from the returning, repenting soul who has at last felt the Father's arms around his neck and the Father's warm kisses on his cheek and is sitting down at the table where the happy household eat and drink and are merry. The time of praising has come indeed when the time of finding has arrived. Happy day! Happy day, when we meet with God in Jesus Christ!

Now, dear soul, the promise secures that you will find God in Christ because the promise is that you will praise Him, and you cannot praise Him until you have found His grace and favor in Christ. Therefore, I am sure you will enjoy salvation before long. Oh, it is not to be thought of that a soul should seek God and not find Him. Imagine the penitent Prodigal Son seeking his father, reaching his father's house, searching in the chambers of his father's mansion, going into his father's fields, and crying out, "My Father, my Father, I have lost you. Will you not be found by me?" and doing this month after month and year after year and not finding his father after all. There is no such parable as that in Holy Scripture, and there could not be one. It would not be godlike or Christlike. There is nothing like it, as a matter of fact, and there will never be except where unbelief comes in and wickedly misrepresents the Lord.

My God, in Your universe You think of everything. The beast has its lair, and the seabird has its home. The fish finds its food, and even the insect has a table provided for it. As for Your poor creature, man, though greatly erring, You do not forget him, but You have made us wonder that You are so mindful of him, that You have such tender regard for him and visit him so graciously. It is not possible that any one of all Your creatures could seek You like a child who cries for its mother in the dark and not find You after all. You are not far from any of us.

God may try you. He may let you wait a while before He grants you the comforts of realized pardon. There may be something about you, especially your unbelief, that prevents you from finding Him, but He must be found by you. He will be before long.

Suppose you have a child who has done wrong, but who, with many tears, comes to you and says, "Father, forgive me"? Will you not forgive? You know that for a while you may chide him and say,

"The offense is great. It has been often repeated. I cannot readily pass by it this time." But if you see your child still weeping and still imploring your favor with a broken heart, do you not long to say, "My child, I have forgiven and forgotten your fault"? You know you do, and if you, *"being evil"* (Matt. 7:11), know how to forgive your children, how much more will your heavenly Father give pardon and free grace to those who seek Him? You *"shall praise the LORD that seek him."* Lay hold of that promise.

## We Will Go On Seeking and Praising

When you have found Him to the joy of your heart, the promise of the text will be fulfilled in a third sense. Seeking the Lord is sometimes used in Scripture as the equivalent of true religion, and it very aptly describes it, for our life consists of endeavoring to know the Lord more and more. Now, since Christ has died, true religion is praise. The genius of the Christian religion is joy. Its proper spirit is delight, and its highest exercise is praise. *"They shall praise the LORD that seek him."*

Now we go up to the house of the Lord with the congregation of the faithful with songs of holy joy. Now we draw near to the feast of communion at the Lord's table with delight, and before we depart, we sing a hymn. Now we go forth to the good fight of faith, and our battle song is a jubilant psalm. Now we even go to our beds of painful sickness and sing the Lord's high praises there. Since Jesus died, our heaviness is dead; our murmuring is buried in His tomb. Since Jesus endured the wrath of God, which was due to us, that wrath has passed away forever, and it is now the privilege and, even more so, the duty of every Christian to rejoice in the Lord. Let all the people praise Him, and let the redeemed of the Lord be foremost in the joy.

## We Will See Him in Heaven

We will then praise the Lord, those of us who seek Him, in another day and another state of being, when we will be in another place. What praises will you and I pour forth then! There are reasons why I consider myself to have been the greatest debtor to God of any man who ever lived. I can see special ways in which I was undeserving and special mercies on the part of God towards me. I am obligated to praise the name of the Lord more ardently than anyone because I am more deeply indebted to His grace. Everyone can, I have no doubt, enter into the same vein of thought, and not without reason. You will feel as if you have the greatest reason to magnify His blessed name when you find yourself seated among the blood-washed, and holding the palm branch of eternal victory. Oh, what a song will go up then; what shouts of those who triumph and songs of those who feast will make heaven's high arches ring in that glad day when *"they shall praise the LORD that seek him"*!

What a promise this is. I leave it in your hands, only remarking that it takes the most delightful shape possible, because if you are a true seeker, the thing you want above all things is to be able to glorify God. You desire to be pardoned and to be renewed in heart with this objective in mind: that you may be able to render acceptable praise to Him whom you have offended. Well, that is the very blessing that is promised to you, *"They shall praise the LORD that seek him."* It includes, of course, the removal from your heart of everything that would prevent you from praising Him and the breaking down of every barrier that would keep you back from joining the celestial choirs who, day without night, with their eternal symphonies, circle His throne rejoicing.

## THE PRAISE

*"They shall praise the LORD that seek him."* What will the praise be about? What will be the subject of the song? Now I have before me an utterly endless task, if I am to catalogue the subjects of praise for a soul when it has found peace with God.

### That We Found Him As We Did

Some of you found Him so readily. You only heard a sermon, and that one sermon led you to Christ. Others of us did not find Him so soon or so easily, and yet we found Him in the very nick of time. Just when we were going to lie down in despair, when Satan suggested that no hope remained, then man's hopelessness was God's opportunity, and we found the Lord exactly at the best moment. Blessed be His name!

Oh, to find Him at all! How great a reward! If a man should lie a thousand years in the prison of despair, but should find Christ in the end, it would be worthwhile to have suffered the thousand years of daily death. If we may at last say, "My God, my God," with unfaltering tongue and a heart that knows it is reconciled to Him, we will make it our heaven to praise Him with all our might.

### That We Found Such a Savior

It is possible to see the Lord as being on the cross and uttering this promise, *"They shall praise the LORD that seek him."* When we find the Lord, we always find Him in Christ upon the cross, and the Atonement becomes a chief feature of our joy.

Do you remember the first time you saw, by faith, the incarnate God bearing human sin, when that grand doctrine of substitution flashed on your soul like the first sight of the sun to a man who had been blind? Do you remember when you first really knew that God laid on Christ your iniquities, and that He was punished instead of you so that you cannot by any possibility be punished, for it is unjust to exact the penalty for one offense twice? Did you ever get the glory of that light concentrated on your soul, so that you knew for sure that God for Christ's sake had forgiven you and justly forgiven you, because of the blood of Jesus? Did you ever drink in the meaning of those words, *"faithful and just to forgive us our sins"* (1 John 1:9)?

If so, then I know that after the first overwhelming impression of intense delight, you did praise God, and you have not stopped doing so, for there is enough in that one simple fact to cause you to praise God throughout the ages of eternity. Salvation by substitution so satisfies the conscience that it fills the heart with overflowing delight.

The love I prize is righteous love,
Inscribed on the sin-bearing tree;
Love that exacts the sinner's debt,
Yet, in exacting sets him free.

Love that condemns the sinner's sin,
Yet, in condemning, pardon seals;
That saves from righteous wrath, and yet
In saving, righteousness reveals.

This is the love that calms my heart,
That soothes each conscience-pang within,
That pacifies my guilty dread,
And frees me from the power of sin.

Oh, to think that such a one as Jesus should be our Savior, that heaven's Darling should condescend to assume our nature and become bone of our bone and flesh of our flesh! To think that He would live such a life and die such a death, that He would present to God a work so perfect, without flaw, without excess! Is there not room for praises here? Now we are clean before the Lord because we have been washed in Christ's blood. Yes, we are as pure as if we had never sinned. Standing arrayed in Christ's righteousness, we are even more righteous than Adam before the Fall, for he had only a human righteousness, but we have a divine righteousness. In Christ Jesus, the Second Adam, we are nearer to God than if we had been born of the first Adam while untainted by sin.

Now, there is a man who is like God—Jesus, our brother—who is also very God of very God. Man is exalted to the highest conceivable degree in the person of Jesus Christ, and we have become heirs of

God, joint heirs with Jesus Christ. As the seeking
soul learns more and more of this, he praises God
more and more. Is it not so? Does your soul not bless
the Savior? Yes, and the longer we live and the more
we know about the Lord, the more we find reasons
for extolling Him. Indeed, everything around us,
within us, and above us seems to suggest a reason
for blessing His name.

### That We Have Security

Many a song has been poured from my soul as I
have remembered that my Lord has given me a life
that cannot die. I have rejoiced because He has written me on His heart, from where my name can never
be erased. I have praised Him because He has made
a covenant with me, to which He has pledged His
honor and His word, and which He has sealed with
His blood. My joy has flowed out as I have recalled
that I am His child, and that He never did and never
can tear from His heart's love even the least of His
children. The mountains may depart and the hills be
removed, but the covenant of His peace can never be
removed (Isa. 54:10), as He has declared.

> My name from the palms of his hands,
>     Eternity cannot erase;
> Impressed on his heart it remains
>     In marks of indelible grace.
>
> Yes, I to the end shall endure.
>     As sure as the earnest is given;
> More happy but not more secure
>     The glorified spirits in heaven.

There is abundant raw material for praise in all this. Where can you find better? *"They shall praise the LORD that seek him."*

## That We Ever Sought the Lord at All

Think what it was that made us seek Him; what was it but sovereign grace? What moistened our eyes with the first tear of repentance? What brought from our souls the first sigh of desire for Christ? What, I say, but grace? And where did that grace come from but from His eternal purpose, which He planned through Christ Jesus before the world existed? And where did that purpose come from but from His divine sovereignty, even as it is written, *"I will have mercy on whom I will have mercy, and I will have compassion on whom I will have compassion"* (Rom. 9:15). Therefore, let us glorify His holy name and not think of works or merits or anything in man that could have won for us the love of the Most High. Boasting is excluded, but praise is secured. Give all the glory to His holy name forever and forever, and let the text stand true in your case, *"They shall praise the LORD that seek him."*

## Let Us Praise the Lord

If these things are so, even we who have already sought and found Him can praise Him. If our poor friends the seekers are soon to bless His name, let us show them the way. We sought and we found; let us magnify the Lord at once. Do you think we praise our heavenly Father half enough? Do we not rob Him of His glory by getting down in the dumps and giving way to care and perhaps to murmuring? This is not the right spirit for a Christian. Where there is so much undeserved mercy, there ought to be more grateful joy.

Do you think we are demonstrative enough in our praise? I am sure we are not. Few around us would ever dream that we are half as favored as we are. Do we sing one-tenth as much as Christians ought to sing? We hum a tune now and then, very quietly, but we are terribly afraid of being heard and of annoying people. I do not find the frivolous world much afraid of annoying us with their songs; do they not wake us up at night with their lewd discords? If we were half as earnest as we ought to be, we would sometimes at least make the streets ring with the praises of God. It would be well to be a little indiscreet occasionally, and now and then provoke the charge of fanaticism, for this would be one proof of earnest sincerity. Once, at least, in our lives we should let our Lord ride through the streets again in public triumph amid our own most hearty enthusiasm, until Pharisees rebuke us and say, *"Hearest thou what these say?"* (Matt. 21:16).

Oh, for this love let rocks and hills
　　Their lasting silence break;
And all harmonious human tongues
　　Their Savior's praises speak.

Yes, and all inharmonious tongues, too. Let all creatures that have breath praise the Lord.

Yes we will praise thee dearest Lord,
　　Our souls are all on flame.

Hosanna round the spacious earth
To thine adored name!

May the Lord set our hearts on fire. May we be full of triumphant praise, marching on with hosannas and hallelujahs, magnifying, praising, and extolling the Lord, whom we sought in the hour of trouble and whom we found in the day of His grace.

## Chapter 5

## Wholehearted Seeking

*"And ye shall seek me, and find me, when ye shall
search for me with all your heart."*
—Jeremiah 29:13

In the preceding chapter, I gave comforting words
to those who seek the Lord, dwelling upon those
encouraging words of Psalm 22: *"They shall praise
the LORD that seek him."* I therefore desire to follow
up that discussion by another in which I will distin-
guish between those who truly seek and those who
only nominally seek the Lord. Such a distinction will
be useful in many ways.

Perhaps, dear friend, after reading the previous
chapter, you said, "I do not understand this promise
that seekers will praise God, for I have been seeking
for months but I have not been able to praise Him
yet. Surely the promise cannot be true of me." Rest
assured, dear friend, that the promise is true to you
if you are true to it. The Word of the Lord is sure.
There can be no question about that point. The
questions to be raised must deal with yourself and
your searching. Either you are not seeking or else
you are seeking in the wrong way.

Always conclude that if a general promise does not turn out to be true in your particular instance, there is something in you that hinders it. You must have fallen short of the character needed for the promise to be fulfilled. The promise itself cannot be suspected. *"Let God be true, but every man a liar"* (Rom. 3:4). You may consider why you have not obtained a certain blessing that you have asked for by any theory that humbles you, but you must never suppose that the Lord will break His promise. If the Lord were to break His promise, it would dishonor His holy name, deny His faithfulness, and pour contempt upon His truth. If His good Word appears to fail regarding you, is there not a cause? Does not sin lie at the door (Gen. 4:7)? Is there not some idol in the inner room that must be searched for and taken away? *"Are the consolations of God small with thee? is there any secret thing with thee?"* (Job 15:11).

It is a general truth that proper food will build up the human frame, but if food is eaten, and yet no nourishment whatever is obtained from it, we conclude that the system has been thrown out of order by some inward disease. The meat is good; it therefore must be the stomach or some other organ that is ailing and is turning that which is good into evil.

If a fire is lit and a person is placed close to it, yet he declares that he is not warmed by the heat, we do not, because of this, entertain any doubt concerning the power of fire to warm the human body. We conclude that the person has a fever or some other malady that prevents him from feeling the natural warmth of the fire. The failure of warmth cannot lie in the fire. It must be in the person, for fire must warm any healthy limbs that are held near to it.

If a medicine that has been known to produce a cure in hundreds of cases is taken by an individual and is found to have no result, or to work in a manner contrary to its natural and ordinary effect, we conclude that either the state of the case has been badly judged or that there is some other potent drug present that neutralizes its effect. The person himself may not be aware that he is eating or imbibing something that is counteracting the prescription of his physician, yet it may be so. Therefore, the medicine is not to be distrusted, but the interposing substance must bear all the blame.

For these reasons I will try to differentiate a little, with no wish at all to grieve any seeking soul, but with a strong desire to indicate any weak point in the seeking, any counteracting habit that may be at this time preventing the soul from entering at once into the peace and joy for which he is seeking. *"He that seeketh findeth"* (Matt. 7:8) is an indisputable fact, but since all that glitters is not gold, so all that bears the name is not seeking.

The verse tells us: *"Ye shall seek me, and find me, when ye shall search for me with all your heart."* Wholeheartedness is the quality required. Later, I will show the reasons why wholeheartedness is required and indicate one or two of the main hindrances to it, which we pray that the Lord will remove.

## THE QUALITIES OF EVERY TRUE SEEKER

Having the required wholeheartedness means that the seeker must search for the Lord with all his heart. This means the following things.

## Having an Undivided Object

See how the text reads: *"Ye shall seek me, and find me, when ye shall search for me with all your heart."* There is one and only one object in this. The sinner is at a distance from God, and guilt divides him from his God. He longs to draw near and to be reconciled to the heavenly Father. He therefore seeks God, and God alone. *"My soul thirsteth for God, for the living God"* (Ps. 42:2). *"Oh that I knew where I might find him!"* (Job 23:3).

Now, the guilty person will find the Lord only in Christ Jesus, who is the mercy seat where God meets sinners and hears their prayers. It is there that the fullness of the Godhead dwells bodily, and there the fullness of divine grace and truth is stored up so that we may receive from it. We must turn our eyes, then, to God in Christ Jesus, and keep them fixed there. *"My soul, wait thou only upon God; for my expectation is from him"* (Ps. 62:5). If we are not sincere in looking towards Christ and in our desire of salvation through Him, it will be no wonder if we seek mercy but seek in vain. How can a man run in two ways at the same time?

Seeker, you must shake off all trust in self, for God will have none of it. You must not seek God by the works of the law or by any supposed merit that is or ever can be in yourself, for He utterly refuses this. If you attempt to mix law with Gospel, self with Christ, and merit with mercy, you will certainly miss your mark. Your whole soul must concentrate on this: to find God as He is revealed in Christ, a God of grace and love, the God who justifies the ungodly when He looks on the merit of His Son and sees the sinner's confidence in Him.

You must seek the Lord in such a way that you will make no provision for the lusts of the flesh and the desires of the mind. If it costs you giving up every pleasure that you have in order to seek the Lord, you must seek Him so entirely that you would cut off right arms and pluck out right eyes sooner than you would miss Him, and so miss eternal life. However sweet the sin may have been to your palate, you must cast it out of your mouth, for it is as poisonous as it is pleasant, and therefore is to be put far away from you. *"Make not provision for the flesh, to fulfil the lusts thereof"* (Rom. 13:14), for if you do, you have not sought the Lord with all your heart. There must be one object, and that must be neither self nor sin. You must feel and say, *"In God is my salvation and my glory: the rock of my strength, and my refuge, is in God'* (Ps. 62:7); therefore, with strong desire I follow after the Lord, even the Lord alone."

Moreover, there must be no reservations during this search to gratify pride in any of its shapes. If you say within your heart, "I will only accept mercy if it comes to me in a certain way," you put yourself out of all hope of grace, for God is sovereign and will do as He wills with His own. Some will not have Christ without signs and wonders. They demand singular experiences, horrible depressions, or delirious excitements, and they will not believe unless some marvelous thing is worked in them or before them.

You must make no conditions with God, either of this or of any other kind. You will find Him, if you will seek Him, without bargains and terms and demands. Who are you that you would demand anything of your Maker and lay down rules and regulations for the dispensing of a mercy to which you have no claim? Come as you are, poor sinner, and without any reservation submit yourself to the mercy of God in Christ Jesus, only desiring this one thing: that you may find God and His love in Christ Jesus.

> Lord, deny me what thou wilt,
> Only ease me of my guilt;
> Suppliant at thy feet I lie,
> Give me Christ, or else I die.

You will find the Lord to be your help and your salvation, if you seek Him as the one sole object of your desire. *"One thing have I desired of the LORD, that will I seek after"* (Ps. 27:4).

### Seeking with All Your Faculties

A man must seek God in Christ Jesus with his entire nature, as the text says, *"with all your heart."* David said, *"My soul thirsteth for thee, my flesh longeth for thee"* (Ps. 63:1). If one part of the man refuses to seek the Lord and remains reserved for Satan, then the Evil One has a lien on the whole man. Imagine a little bird: it tries to fly into the open air, but it is not free. And why not? Its wings are loose; see how it flutters. Its head is not bound; hear how it sings. One foot is free, too. Why is it not at liberty? Do you not perceive that the other leg is bound by a thin twine? True, it is only held by that single thread, but yet it is not free. The whole bird is bound because that one foot is held by that single thread. Likewise, as long as a man of free choice gives up any part of himself to the power of sin and keeps back any part of his nature from seeking God, he is not really seeking the Lord at all, but rather he remains a slave to sin.

If you want to find God, set your faculties on the search, marshal your powers, muster your forces, and let your entire nature, body, soul, and spirit, search for Jesus Christ as the *"merchant man, seeking goodly pearls"* (Matt. 13:45). Set your thoughts at work, and let them search the Scriptures. Arouse your understanding, and endeavor to comprehend your danger and to know your remedy. Set your wits to work. Let your ingenuity and your research be brought to bear on heavenly things, for maybe when you do understand the Gospel you will believe and have peace. An enlightened judgment is a great help towards faith.

Many a man remains without peace because his understanding has never been exercised upon the Gospel and divine things. If he would think them over, meditate upon them, and ponder them in his heart, new light would flash into his soul by the enlightening of the sacred Spirit, and he would see and believe. *"Understandest thou what thou readest?"* (Acts 8:30) is an important question and suggests that, in the search for salvation, the understanding should be called into play. Do not expect to be saved as dumb, driven cattle, but as a reasonable man. Therefore, use your reason and understanding on divine things, asking the Lord to teach your reason the right reason and to give your understanding a right understanding of His Word.

It will be well for a man in seeking the Lord to use his memory and his conscience. Let him go over the list of his past sins and recall the wanderings of his heart, the follies of his tongue, the iniquities of his hand. Maybe memory will call up conscience and become the mother of repentance. The recollection of the sinful past will, by the Spirit's grace, create a penitent present. Do not forget, I implore you, to remember your former days, for God requires you to do so. Remember, too, what God has done by way of mercy to others. Think of friends and companions who are saved. Remember the grand old records of inspiration; turn to the Bible and see how God has saved seeking souls, and your memory may thus work faith in you by the Spirit of God. The text commands you to search *"with all your heart,"* and your memory, as one of the faculties of your mind, should assist in the search.

As for your will, how necessary it is that this also is captured and compelled to join heartily in the pursuit. It is a stubborn thing and will not readily bend, but how can you expect to find mercy if you are not willing to submit to God's rebukes and accept His methods of salvation? Bring forth someone who lives by his own will, and let grace cause him to submit himself. Though he was once proud of his own will, he must bare his neck to the yoke of Christ and acknowledge that the will of the Lord is higher than man's will. Make him say, *"Not as I will, but as thou wilt"* (Matt. 26:39).

As to every other faculty that you have, if you are indeed in earnest, let them be awakened. Do not leave a single part of your nature behind when you come to God, but seek Him with your whole heart, with intense eagerness, and with strong desire.

> *My son, if thou wilt receive my words, and hide my commandments with thee; so that thou incline thine ear unto wisdom, and apply thine heart to understanding; yea, if thou criest after knowledge, and liftest up thy voice for understanding; if thou seekest her as silver, and searchest for her as for hid treasures; then shalt thou understand the fear of the LORD, and find the knowledge of God.   (Prov. 2:1–5)*

### Awakened Energy

*"And ye shall seek me, and find me, when ye shall search for me with all your heart."* Fulfilling this requirement includes getting out of that dull, sluggish, indifferent spirit that seems so common. Indifference to eternal realities seems to impregnate the very air we breathe in this sleepy world—sleepy, I mean, as to things spiritual and divine. We are busy about a thousand things but sluggish about our souls. Yet do not be deceived; if men are to be saved, it will not be accomplished while they slumber, and mercy will not be found by a listless, careless, lackadaisical search for it. No, when the Spirit of God sets a man searching, he becomes earnest, intense, fervent, vehement, and strives to enter in at the narrow gate, for *"the kingdom of heaven suffereth violence, and the violent take it by force"* (Matt. 11:12).

He who wants to be saved must be resolved to escape from the wrath to come. It must come to this with you: that you cannot rest until you find Christ and eternal life. You cannot endure to be damned, and therefore you are determined that if there is on earth or in heaven any remedy for your soul's sickness, you will have it if seeking can obtain it. When the Lord has made you thus resolute, you will need to have perseverance, to follow hard after Him until you have beheld His face in peace.

Therefore, if you have once read the Scriptures to find Christ in them, you will read them again and again and dig over the field of the Word ten times until you find the hidden treasure. If you have once prayed for grace and peace, you will pray again and again and again and again, until your knees become callused rather than miss the blessing. If you have heard the Word preached many times, and yet it has not brought peace to your soul, you will be early and late in waiting at the posts of Jehovah's doors to hear those glad tidings of which it is written, *"Hear, and your soul shall live"* (Isa. 55:3). There will be in your spirit a determination that cannot be shaken, a desire that cannot be appeased.

We must be importunate, or persistent, like the widow with the unjust judge, or the man at midnight with his friend, for importunity prevails. *"Arise, cry out in the night: in the beginning of the watches pour out thine heart like water before the...Lord"* (Lam. 2:19). If you cannot rest until you receive the kiss of pardon, you will soon obtain it. If you cannot be at ease until you are taken into the Father's house and declared to be His child, you will soon rejoice in the adoption. May the Lord be pleased to stir all seekers to passionate earnestness, for when they are filled with agony of soul they will obtain mercy. If you are content to go without salvation, you will go without it. But if your soul longs, yes, even faints for it, you will have it.

There are some poor souls who will, perhaps, be distressed with these remarks about energetic seeking. They are constitutionally weak and feeble in all that they feel and do. Therefore, they will say, "Sir, I am afraid I never was as earnest as you describe. I am a poor feeble soul and very low in spirit. I fear I have no such eagerness and energy." No, dear trembler, and I would not have you misunderstand me, for the force I am now commending is not physical but spiritual, and rather that of weakness than of strength.

Have you not heard that once upon a time two knocks were given at mercy's door? He who kept the door opened to one in an instant, but to the other there was no reply. The knock to which the door was opened was but a gentle one and scarcely could be heard by those outside the gate, yet it evidently struck some secret spring on the door, for the sound of it thundered along the palace halls. The second knock was very loud and was heard by all who stood around the door, but it commanded no answer from within.

He who had knocked loudly marveled and inquired of him who kept the gate, "How is it that I have knocked so loudly and yet have not entered, while the trembling woman whose knock was very soft and low obtained immediate admittance?" Then he who kept the door answered, "She who knocked so feebly, knocked with all her might. Her strength was little, but it was all she had, and therefore it sounded powerfully within these palace walls. As for you, you have put forth much energy, but it was not your all. Therefore, there is no response to you. Take the gate's knocker with both of your hands, and throw your whole soul into each blow, and see if the door does not yield admittance to you." He did so, and the gate flew open to him. He entered into the place that his feeble sister had already gained. If you seek God with all your heart, no matter if your heart is strong or feeble, you will find Him.

## THE REASON FOR THIS REQUIREMENT

The requirement is so natural that it needs no apology. It must recommend itself to every thoughtful person. However, it may help us to be earnest if we are told why it is required of us. It is required for the following reasons.

### Wholeheartedness Is Required in Every Worthy Pursuit

I knew a man who had a business, but if you called to see him about any matter, you seldom found him at his office. He was taking a holiday, or else he had not risen. He made an appointment with you, but he never kept it or came in so late that you were weary with waiting. Commissions that he was entrusted with were often left undone or attended to in a slovenly manner. Do you wonder that when I passed by his shop one day I saw that it was closed and learned that he had failed? Do you not know that success in life depends upon earnestness in it? Do you not teach your children this important lesson? And if it is so in the lower things of this mortal life, how much more is it in the matters of the world to come?

## Wholehearted Seeking

No man becomes learned by sleeping with a book for his pillow, or famous by slumbering at the foot of the ladder of honor. You find everywhere that the kingdom of this world *"suffereth violence"* (Matt. 11:12) and never more so than in these days of increasing competition. Surely you cannot expect that if you must run for this world you may creep and win the next! No, no. You, seeker, will find the Lord if you seek Him with all your heart, and by no other way. Spiritual sluggards will starve. Labor, therefore, for the meat that endures to eternal life.

### The Danger Is So Great

Consider for a moment the imminence of your peril and the overwhelming nature of it. The unsaved man lies under the wrath of God, and if a man only knew what the wrath of God is, he would think that Nebuchadnezzar's furnace was cool compared with that burning oven. He is in instant danger of death and of the Judgment, and of that second death that follows on the heels of condemnation and consists of banishment from the presence of God and the glory of His power. Oh, if a man only knew while he lived what it is to die—if he could only guess what it is to stand before God's court, and if he could have an inkling of what it must be to be cast where the worm does not die and the fire is not quenched (Isa. 66:24)—this would surely make him seek the Lord with all his heart.

Oh, seeker, if you were in a burning house, you would be eager to get out of it. If it seemed that you would sink in a river, you would struggle desperately to get to shore. How is it then that you are so little moved by the peril of your soul? Man is awakened once he knows his life is in peril; how much more earnest ought he to be when eternal life or eternal death are the solemn alternative! *"What meanest thou, O sleeper? arise, call upon thy God"* (Jonah 1:6).

### The Greatness of God's Mercy

God's mercy is none other than pardon of all your sins, perfect righteousness in Christ Jesus, safety through His precious blood, adoption into the family of God, and eternal enjoyment of the presence of God in heaven. They who seek pearls and gold and precious stones use all their eyes and all their wits, but what are those gaudy toys compared with these immortal treasures? How ought a man to seek heaven and eternal life? Should it not be with all his heart?

### The Earnestness of All Involved

Poor seeker, everyone concerned with this matter is in earnest. Look down on hell's domain, and see how earnest Satan is to hold you and to ruin you! How diligently the Enemy baits his hooks and sets his traps to catch the souls of men! How he does encircle the sea and land to hold his captives, for fear that they may escape!

See how earnest, on the other hand, Christ is. He proved His earnestness by a life of toil by day and of prayer by night, by hunger and thirst and faintness and bloody sweat. The zeal of God's house had eaten Him up. He was earnest, even to the death, for sinners.

And God is in earnest; there is no mockery with Him, or carelessness or indifference about human souls. When He speaks of sinners perishing, He cries out with a solemn oath that He has no pleasure in their death, but if they refuse His love and defy His justice to the last, He will not trifle with them—He will judge and punish in earnest. Has He not said, *"Consider this, ye that forget God, lest I tear you in pieces, and there be none to deliver"* (Ps. 50:22). The majesty of His power is revealed in flaming wrath against transgressors. Hell is no trifle, and His wrath is no small matter.

Heaven and hell, then, are in earnest, and so must you be if you want to find salvation. Will we who have to tell you to escape from the wrath to come pray to be in earnest ourselves? Will we never feel earnest enough but always cry that we may be seized with a yet more intense passion for your welfare? Will it seem to you that salvation is an ordinary matter, a thing that you may let alone and let happen as it may? Oh, seekers, if you talk in this way, the madness of sin is very manifest in you. May the Lord make you sane.

## You Have Been Earnest Enough in the Ways of Sin

Think of yourself as engrossed with those things of which you ought to be ashamed. Have you not been earnest indeed there? Concerning this world: you have risen early and have sat up late and have eaten the bread of carefulness, as opposed to the *"bread of idleness"* (Prov. 31:27). When you went into sin, did you not sin with both your hands?

Perhaps there are some reading this who could never sin enough. When they were with others, they were ahead of all of them—ringleaders in every sort of wickedness. It was not enough for them to be common sinners, but they were known by everybody to be the boldest and most daredevil of all the crew. They led the caravan in the march to hell. And, are you going to manifest all that earnestness in reviling and rebelling against God, but have no warmth, no ardor, no strong excitement when you seek the Lord and His grace? Think of this, and scold your apathetic steps!

### Seeking Must Be Wholehearted to Be Genuine

Suppose there is a man who almost repents of his sin or half repents of it. Does this not mean that he does not repent of it at all? How can there be repentance of a deed to which half the heart is still wedded? If only half the heart seems to be separated from sin, it is merely a semblance of true repentance. The man's whole heart still truly loves his sin. And how can there be halfhearted faith? He who half believes does not believe at all.

If you say, "I almost believe," where is your faith? *"If thou believest with all thine heart, thou mayest"* (Acts 8:37) be baptized and added to the church. But if you believe halfheartedly, what sort of faith is this? For a man to turn half from sin and half to God—is that conversion? No, he who has turned only halfway to God has not turned to God at all. He remains where he is, only he has probably added hypocrisy to his other sins. He who leaves half his heart behind him when he comes to God does not come at all. *"Their heart is divided; now shall they be found faulty"* (Hos. 10:2).

## The Christian Life Is Impossible without Wholeheartedness

Hear how true Christians pray. Do they pray with half their hearts? No, for one has said, *"with my whole heart have I sought thee"* (Ps. 119:10). So say all sincere believers. They know that if they ask in a chilly style they are asking to be denied, and therefore they besiege heaven with all the power of prayer. They knock and knock again with fervor and perseverance when they want to obtain what they need. They say with wrestling Jacob, *"I will not let thee go, except thou bless me"* (Gen. 32:26). Prayer is the vital breath of the Christian, and if he cannot pray without wholeheartedness, then it is clear that to have spiritual life, you, seeker, must give all your heart to it.

Obedience to God in the believer is wholehearted. What did David say? *"I will keep thy precepts with my whole heart"* (Ps. 119:69). There is no doing the will of God with half a heart. That would be a kind of obedience that He could not in any way accept. It would be a sign of formality and hypocrisy, but not of sincerity. Genuine Christians love God with all their hearts. What is the demand of the old law but, *"Thou shalt love the Lord thy God with all thy heart, and with all thy soul"* (Matt. 22:37)? To love God with half your heart would be another name for not loving God at all. Love for God is the proof and test of a believer, but how can you have it if even in your seeking your heart is divided?

When believers praise God, they do it in the style of the psalmist who said, *"I will praise thee, O*

LORD, *with my whole heart"* (Ps. 9:1). What other songs can have music in them to appeal to the ears of the God of truth? All ten-stringed instruments must be vain if the heart does not praise. *"Unite my heart to fear thy name"* (Ps. 86:11), said the holy man, and we must pray the same, for the Christian life is impossible without wholeness of heart.

Only imagine for a moment that I were permitted to say to you, "God is very easily entreated, and if you seek Him, no matter in what cold and careless way, He will be found by you. You may be half asleep, but yet as long as there is a little desire in your soul, it will go well with you. You do not need to be very earnest or especially prayerful or whole-hearted. You may take it very easy, and it will all go well with you." What pretty teaching that would be! Some might like it, but what sort of Christians would we produce by it?

Even when we teach earnestness, a great number of professing Christians are quite drowsy. However, what would they be if we had such a slumbering gospel as this to teach? I have known people to go to sleep in the house of prayer when the seats have been hard, but suppose we provided pillows and velvety cushions for drowsy heads? Who would wonder if they all went to sleep? What sort of a church would we build up if we did not implore the inquirer to seek with his whole heart but urged him to be indifferent from the very first? Have I not reduced the whole thing to an absurdity, and do you not see at once that there must be a seeking of the Lord with all your heart if indeed you are ever to find Him? May the divine Spirit, who comes as a rushing mighty wind and as a consuming fire, come upon all wavering hearts right now and cause them to be eager for the things that will bring them peace.

## THE HINDRANCES TO THIS REQUIREMENT

### Presumption

The ungodly say within themselves, "God is very merciful and ready to forgive. We like to hear the abundant mercy of God proclaimed. We are pleased to hear how willing the Father is to forgive, and how He delights to receive returning prodigals." Yes, and after saying this, they continue in sin. Their low, cowardly, worse-than-brutish hearts resolve to sin because God is merciful! I do not know how to find adjectives sufficiently strong to describe the degradation of a nature that can multiply offenses because the offended One has a forgiving spirit.

How worse than brutish are you who say, "Because God is so merciful, therefore I will go on in sin!" Are you not ashamed of yourself? I am sure I am ashamed of you that such a thought would ever dwell in your mind. It is so ungrateful, so ungenerous. I was going to say it is so devilish, but the Devil himself has never been guilty of this, for he has never had any hope of mercy. To sin because of mercy is a step lower than even the Devil has descended. Because God is merciful, therefore you will not seek His mercy, but will continue in sin? Ah, be ashamed and cursed!

You hear preachers continually say that whoever believes in Jesus is not condemned, and you say to yourself in the secret of your heart, "This is very easy. Only believe, and you will be saved. Simply put your confidence in Christ." You think this is a license to go on in sin. Let me put this to you again so that you may see the baseness of such a course. Do you say, "Because the way of salvation is so simple, I will not attend to it at present. Any day will do. I will put it off"?

Oh, can it be that you have fallen as low as this? Oh, the deep depravity of your spirit, that if God is so ready to forgive, you are, therefore, all the more unready to be forgiven, and because He provides it on such easy terms, you therefore turn on your heel and refuse His love. What is this but virtually to crucify Christ afresh by sinning because He is gracious? What is this but mocking Him and spitting in His face by refusing His salvation because it is so free? Oh, do not do this! Do not be so unmanly, so cruel to yourself, and so ungenerous to the Christ of God.

"Ah," says one, "a few words of prayer at the end will do."

> While the lamp holds out to burn,
> The vilest sinner may return.

I have often wondered how men can venture to speak thus within themselves. They seldom talk like that to others because they do not dare, but they flatter themselves in secret. How do you know that you will have the few minutes in which to utter those pious words? *"God be merciful to me a sinner"* (Luke 18:13) may be more than you will be able to say. Beware, for fear that He will take you away with a stroke, for then you will not be able to raise even the shortest prayer.

Some have been stricken down in their sins, and those have been the very men who said, "Anytime will do. I can turn to God when I please and make my peace with Him." Many men have fallen from a height or been killed in a train wreck or drowned at sea or seized with a stroke, and their souls have stood in all their naked shame before the court of God to answer for their ungodly speeches. Presumption upon the mercy of God is the reason why so many wrap themselves up in the garments of carnal security and put far from them the evil day. God deliver you from this great evil!

### The Remains of Self-confidence

If many knew that they could not save themselves, they would be in earnest to seek God and His righteousness, but they still harbor some vain notion that there must be at least a little good thing about them—at least a spark, and a great fire may come from a spark. They never were as bad as some: they were not drunkards, and they did not swear. They have never plunged into actual lust and defiled themselves with uncleanness. Somewhere or other they have accumulated a little store of natural goodness, and upon this they dote in a timid, half-suspicious way.

Therefore, they do not cry out to God with the energy of those who must find mercy in Christ or be forever lost. He who thinks that he can swim will never seize the life preserver with the clutch of a drowning man. How fierce is the grasp of a man who is drowning and knows that his tight grip is his only chance! He clutches so hard that his fingers could break through a wooden board. When a man feels that nothing is left to him but God in Christ, then with earnestness he seizes upon the hope set before him.

### Despair

Some of you do not believe that you can be forgiven. You imagine that you can never be God's people. If you were quite sure that you could obtain perfect peace with God—if you knew that before the sun goes down today, you might have the bright eye that looks up to heaven and says, "There is a place there for me," and the peaceful heart that feels perfect rest in Christ—if you knew that these could be yours, would you not seek them? Well now, I just want to direct you to a verse that comes from the same chapter as our text, and I pray that the Holy Spirit will apply its comfortable assurance to your soul: *"For I know the thoughts that I think toward you, saith the LORD, thoughts of peace, and not of evil"* (Jer. 29:11). Oh, if God's thoughts towards you are good, come to Him now and kiss His feet. The Prodigal, when he was returning home, did not doubt that his father would receive him somehow or other, even if it were as one of his hired servants. He knew that he would be received somehow, and he was willing to be received in any way.

Come, poor soul, the Lord will receive you, whoever you may be. If you consent at once to trust the Lord Jesus with your whole heart, He will receive you. Yes, He will show you how to trust. He will give you faith and give you the blessing that your faith looks for. Why should you not meet your Lord after reading this? Why should you not breathe the prayer of faith and lean your weight upon the Cross of

Christ and find the mercy that our text declares you will find if you seek it with all your heart?

## The Conduct of Professing Christians

Lastly, I am afraid that some people have been kept from wholehearted seeking by the conduct of professing Christians. Let me urge you never to take your example—you who are coming to Christ—from those who profess to be His followers, for some of them are a sorry lot. Yet no matter how bad they are, what is that to you? You have your own soul to look after, and you have to seek Christ with all the more earnestness because some who think that they have found Him have been mistaken.

It is a great pity when there are Christian people around, or those who say that they are Christians, to whom a poor seeking soul is unable to appeal because he would get no sympathy from them. I heard of one who, being ill, desired someone to visit him occasionally and pray with him. A young man, a professing Christian, was mentioned as one who would willingly do so. "No," said the other, "I do not want him to pray with me, for his life does not exemplify prayer."

There are many people of that sort about. One would not have much faith in their prayers or derive much comfort from their conversation, though one may charitably hope that there may be grace in them. It is like coal in a pit—a long way down and hard to get at. Their hearts are lukewarm at best, and therefore they never boil over with warm and loving expressions. The genuine and healthy Christian is one who is so full of love that his heart boils over with good will and others are compelled to feel that the fire of God is burning in his soul, for they see and feel the effects.

Oh, Christians, I trust that you will see to this, because, if you are halfhearted, the chill that surrounds you will freeze the hearts of many who are seeking the Savior. Father, mother, do you not fear that you are hindering your children? Sunday school teachers, if you go to your classes like blocks of ice, you will have cold attention when you come to talk of Christ. If the minister preaches with icicles hanging on his lips, how can he expect that men's hearts will be thawed by his icy words? No, we who are His people must set the example of seeking God with our whole hearts. Then God by the Holy Spirit will bless our examples to others, and they will come to seek Him with their whole hearts, too.

May the Lord cause us to be absolutely earnest, so that we may hope that He will fulfill that ancient promise in us:

> *I will give them one heart, and one way, that they may fear me for ever, for the good of them, and of their children after them: and I will make an everlasting covenant with them, that I will not turn away from them, to do them good; but I will put my fear in their hearts, that they shall not depart from me. Yea, I will rejoice over them to do them good, and I will plant them in this land assuredly with my whole heart and with my whole soul.        (Jer. 32:39–41)*

Think of God blessing us in this way, with His whole heart and His whole soul. Amen, Lord, let it be so.

## Chapter 6

# "Consider Him"

*"For consider him that endured such contradiction of sinners against himself, lest ye be wearied and faint in your minds."*
—Hebrews 12:3

When the Hebrew Christians were suffering dire persecution, the apostle could suggest no better support for their faith than this, *"Consider him."* He directed them to look to Jesus and compare their case with that of their Lord. Such contemplations would prove to be an excellent balm for their distressed minds. A consideration of our Lord and Master is the best conceivable stay and support during persecution. Let us look into that fact.

### CONSIDER JESUS IN TIMES OF PERSECUTION

The believer under persecution should remember that he is suffering no strange thing but is only enduring that which fell upon his Master before him. Should the disciple expect to be above his Lord? *"If they have called the master of the house Beelzebub, how much more shall they call them of his*

131

*household?"* (Matt. 10:25). If those who persecute us had received Christ, they would have received us, but since they reject both Christ and His sayings, the followers of Christ must expect that both their persons and their doctrines will be lightly esteemed.

Remember that in addition to being our Master, Jesus is also God. The opposition of mankind to God, whom it was bound to reverence for every true and just reason, was shamefully unrighteous, yet He endured the antagonism of sinners against Himself with almighty patience. A word from His lips would have withered them, but, like a sheep before her shearers, He was dumb (Isa. 53:7). One glance of His eye of fire would have consumed their spirits, but that eye wept a tear instead. And you are only men. Is it too much that men should mock at you? If God Himself, in the person of His dear Son, has endured the opposition of sinners, who are you that you should wonder, much less should murmur, when you are reviled for Jesus' sake?

Remember, too, that our dear Lord and Master was perfectly innocent. It was a cruel thing that He, who had done no harm to anyone, should be opposed. *"For which of those works do ye stone me?"* (John 10:32), He said. This was a sorrowful question, as much as if He had said, "I have healed your sick, I have fed your hungry, I have raised your dead, and is this the way you repay me! Are stones the only testimonials of your appreciation?" They called Him a drunken man, yet we well know He was temperance itself. They said He had a devil, though He was the Lord of angels. They charged Him with treason, and yet He was Himself the King of Kings and Lord of All.

## "Consider Him"

Now, in us there is much that is evil, and when men falsely speak evil of us, we may say within ourselves, "Ah, if they had known me better, they might have truthfully found fault with me for some other reason." You are not innocent, beloved. Oftentimes you bring the rebuke upon yourselves, and the opposition of sinners against your religion is due to your own fault quite as well as to the world's opposition to the truth that you love. Therefore, if He, the Spotless One, endured, should you who are so far from being innocent not endure also? Should you not be willing to suffer persecution for His sake?

Remember, too, the loving mission for which our Master came. He came into this world on purpose to save men. He had no sinister motive or even a secondary aim. The glory of God in the salvation of lost souls was all He lived for, and despite all that, sinners were infuriated against Him and opposed Him with might and force. Now, the good you can confer upon them is slender enough compared with the rich gifts with which the Master's hands were laden.

You come, it is true, to tell them of a Savior, but you cannot save them. You bring glad tidings of good things, but you are only messengers of the good things your Master actually brought. If they persecuted Him who gave His blood for their redemption, it is not surprising if you, who can only tell of what He has done, should bear some of the reproaches that fell upon Him. Remember, dear friends, how bitter the reproaches that assailed Him were, how the enmity of man put forth all its cruel force. They were not content with slandering Him in life, they needed to hurry Him away to death. Reproach broke His heart, and He was full of heaviness.

Thus they tortured His soul, and you have not forgotten their cruelties to Him in Pilate's hall, where the mental and physical agonies were blended. You cannot forget how He was nailed to the cross and the scorn that greeted Him in the midst of His dying grief. In your battle against sin, you have not yet resisted to the point of having your blood shed. What have you endured compared with Him? As the poet, standing upon the desolate mounds of ruined Rome, considering the death throes of an empire, said, "What are our petty griefs? Let me not number mine," so may you say, "What are the sufferings of any of the believers compared with the infinite griefs of the eternal Son of God." His was suffering indeed. *"Consider him...lest ye be wearied and faint in your minds."*

Yet reflect, beloved, amid all these sufferings, our Lord's temper remained undisturbed. He spoke strong words against hypocrisy and falsehood wherever He encountered them. He spared neither scribe nor Pharisee, but in those stern denunciations not a single atom of personal anger was blended. He did not denounce them out of resentment for their attacks upon Himself but because they deserved to be denounced and were in themselves too vile to be tolerated. No personal animosity ever disturbed the serenity of our great Master's spirit. Moreover, He was never moved to take the slightest revenge on His foes. Even for those who nailed Him to the tree, He had no response but the prayer, *"Father, forgive them; for they know not what they do"* (Luke 23:34).

As He had no vengefulness against them, so they exerted no evil influence upon Him. He persevered in His lifework just as much as if He had never been opposed. Like the sun that goes on in its strength whether there are clouds to hide it or whether it shines out of the blue sky, Christ continued in His heavenward way. He pursued His mighty journey, coming out of His chamber like a bridegroom full of love for his spouse, prepared for the race, not stopping until He had fulfilled His course.

Oh, how strengthening is this contemplation! Let us consider Him and reflect that because of His sufferings and His patience and His forgiveness and His perseverance, He achieved a triumph over evil, which was in effect a complete victory of righteousness over sin. If He could have been provoked, He would have been defeated. If He could have been angered, He would have been overthrown. If He could have been stopped in His progress, then He would not have been victorious. But He bore and bore and bore again. He suffered and suffered, and still He suffered. Like the anvil that does not respond to the hammer, He yet wore out those hammers by His patience.

Consider this, and endure with a patience like your Master's. Consider Jesus, and push on in the allotted path of holy service, just as He did. Consider Him, and look forward with expectancy to the joy of triumphing over evil, for Christ will again get the victory over sin in you. In you He will again be crowned with many crowns, and in you His cross will again become the symbol and weapon of victory.

But, now, I must confess that I did not choose this chapter's text with the idea of discussing it as it stands, but from a light that breaks out of it. I have given you an outline of what could have been said regarding the text. However, the thought occurred to me that if the consideration of Christ is a most effective medicine to the persecuted, to prevent them from being weary or faint in their minds, doubtless the same sacred balm would be beneficial to all other cases of spiritual distress. As I thought of all the diseases of God's people, and like a physician tried this prescription on them, I discovered that it was equally suitable and effective in every case.

## CONSIDER JESUS WHILE SEEKING HIM

I thought this discussion could be directed to those souls that most need care, namely, to those who are seeking Jesus and longing for salvation but who are filled with doubts and despondency. I will say to them, *"Consider him."* I am persuaded, beloved, that if I am enabled by God's Spirit to lead any seeking soul to *"consider him,"* I will also lead that soul into liberty. I believe this topic will be like an opening of the prison doors to those who are bound. I feel that for some of you God has set before you an open door that no man can shut. I will pray over every word that I write, that God may lead you through that open door at the very moment you read these words, so that not twenty or a hundred, but thousands of you may find Christ and be saved with an everlasting salvation. I know the medicine has power in it if God the Holy Spirit will but apply it.

## CONSIDER JESUS IN LIGHT OF YOUR SIN

I now want to appeal to the seeking sinner in simple but earnest language. I say to you who seek salvation, in the name of the living God, consider Christ Jesus, the Son of God, the only Savior of man.

And do this first, in order to face your own examination of your sin. You are awakened enough to know that you have sinned against God. Though a little while ago sin seemed like a trifling matter, you now know that it is a terrible thing, a deadly thing. The thought oppresses your spirit that your sin deserves the wrath of God, that it must be punished, that God would not be a just, moral Governor if He were to pardon you completely without any penalty. He must take vengeance upon your deceit and punish you for your iniquity.

Now, I am glad that you have considered your sin and the heinousness of it, but, poor soul, let me take you by the hand and say to you, *"Consider him"*—the Savior, Christ Jesus. For if you will think of Him, you will remember that God has been just and has laid the sin of His people upon the Lord Jesus Christ. It was impossible that sin should be wiped out with no response from God, but He has been pleased to accept a substitute in the person of His only begotten Son.

Now, the Lord does not need to punish you, sinner, for sin, because He has punished Jesus Christ in the place of all believing sinners. He does not need to punish you with blows, for the lashing you deserve because of your sin, if you believe in Jesus, was laid upon Another's back. Your iniquities were all gathered together in one mighty load and then placed upon the shoulders of Jesus Christ, the great Scapegoat for sin. Does that not remove distress from your mind? If you consider your sin, also consider His five wounds; consider His bloody sweat; consider the tortured person of the immaculate Christ, who was God at the same time that He was man. Say to your soul,

"If Jesus died in your place, a sufficient recompense has been made to the injured honor of God Almighty, so that He can be just and yet the Justifier of the ungodly."

But there rises in your mind this thought, "My sin has placed me in a miserable position, for I am a sinner, and being a sinner I must be obnoxious to the anger of God. It is not possible that a pure God could permit me to dwell in His presence, for He cannot look upon iniquity. How can I hope for acceptance before God when I am defiled?" Now listen, soul. You are a sinner, but *"consider him."* Ask yourself, "Who is Jesus Christ?" I speak with reverence of His name, as our Redeemer. What is He, apart from sinners? Is His name not *"JESUS: for he shall save his people from their sins"* (Matt. 1:21)? If there were no sinners, what could be the value of His name? It would be an empty-sounding title without a meaning. How could He save if there were no lost ones to be saved? He could only be called "Savior" by way of compliment and imagination. Think, why did Jesus come from heaven if He did not have a connection to sinners?

*"This is a faithful saying, and worthy of all acceptation, that Christ Jesus came into the world to save sinners"* (1 Tim. 1:15). He came for nothing if He does not find sinners and save them, and if you and those such as you have no right to look to Jesus, then what did He come to earth for? If there is a righteous man reading this who has no sin, Christ has nothing to do with you; you will perish without the Savior. But if you are a sinner, you are the kind of person that He came to save, and the fact that you know you are a sinner should give you comfort.

Look at who Christ is. *"Consider him."* Is He not a priest? And what is a priest for but to make atonement for the sins of the people? Is our Lord not described as a sacrifice for sin? But for what purpose is there a bloody sacrifice if there is no sin to put away? Jesus is our Advocate. What does the apostle say? *"If any man sin, we have an advocate"* (1 John 2:1). Who wants an advocate with God except a man who has offended? Jesus is an intercessor, too, but who wants Him to intercede for him if he is innocent? He makes intercession for the sins of His people (Rom. 8:34).

You see, then, if you will consider Him, that as the existence of a poor man is necessary before there can be a benefactor, as a disconsolate soul is needful before a comforter can exercise his office, a sinner is necessary before the Savior can be what He is ordained to be. Jesus needs you to be a sinner so that He may exercise His sacred skill upon it. Put a surgeon among men who are never sick, and what is there for him to do? Tell a physician that in a certain city no one is ever ill, and he will leave by the next train. If there were no sinners, what use would a reconciliation be? Therefore, as you consider Him, though your sense of sin will not vanish, your despair about it will be driven quite away.

"Yes, but," says another, "while I have been considering my sin, I have been stunned totally by a sense of its greatness. Oh, sir, mine has not been merely verbal sin. I have committed crimson transgressions of which it is a shame to speak. I have defiled myself by actual crimes that I cannot erase from my memory." That may be true, but I bring you my one remedy: *"Consider him."* What sort of a Savior is Jesus Christ, a little savior or a great one?

Is He not the Son of God, and Himself God? What need is there of a divine person to be an atonement for limited sin? It was the infinity of sin that required the Godhead to become incarnate, in order that human guilt might be put away.

If you say, "I have only a little sin," I tell you Christ will have nothing to do with you. He did not come from heaven to be a physician to a pinprick on a man's finger, which will heal itself, but He is a Physician who delights to heal putrefying sores and gaping wounds and incurable diseases. And you, great, big, devilish sinner, you are just the sort of person whom Christ delights to operate on, for in you He will show His power, His mercy, His grace, and His sovereignty. There is room to display the infinity of His mercy in such a one as you are. Therefore, do not be cast down; do not be faint and weary in seeking Him, but come at once and get close to Him who is mighty to save.

"Yes," says another, "but in examining my sin I see the uniqueness of it. I believe my case stands alone. I do not think another man would have committed the sin I have under the circumstances and with the particular aggravations." That may be. You are a unique sinner, but *"consider him,"* for He is a unique Savior. Was there ever such a one as Jesus? You are a wonderful sinner, but His name is also called *"Wonderful"* (Isa. 9:6). If you are a sinner of such a class as that, and are saved, all the angels will throng the streets of heaven to see you, and will point at you and say, "Behold a monstrous sinner, saved." I say, if it is so, you will bring all the more glory to Christ. You will only make His name even more famous through every heavenly street.

I tell you, however original your sin may be, Christ will meet you. If you have outsoared all others in the daring flights of your sin, Jesus has gone beyond you in the flights of His mercy. Though you might have gone as near to the gates of hell as possible, and have imitated the Devil in his worst qualities, the Redeemer is able to save to the uttermost those who come to God by Him. He is a Savior, and a great one. If you can ever find another Savior like Christ, then I will ask you to find another sinner like yourself. But since you are an unequaled sinner, since you must say of yourself, "There are none worse than I," I will say the same of Jesus: there is none beyond Him. He stands alone and by Himself, and so the sinner and the Savior are well matched. Let your fears be hushed to sleep, and put your trust in Him.

## CONSIDER JESUS IN LIGHT OF GOD'S GREATNESS

Now, the same precious phrase, *"consider him,"* will be useful to the seeking soul, if its contemplation takes another shape. I can well believe that there are those who are grievously oppressed with the sense of the greatness of God. You have lived for years negligent of the God who created you and supplied your needs, but now you have been awakened and aroused to the fact that there is a God, a God whom you have treated hatefully, whom you have shamefully disregarded.

You are now shocked to find that it is so, for now you have a sense of the greatness of God, and you are afraid that He will crush you. You know the justice of God, and you are sure that He must avenge

141

the injuries you have done to His holy law. Therefore, you go about every day with a dreadful sound in
your ears, and you exclaim, "Where will I go from
His presence, and how will I escape from His vengeance?" You are surrounded with God, and in Him
you live and move and have your being. And this
omnipresent God is your enemy, for you have made
Him so by your rebellion against Him.

Now, as a cure for all this, I have to say to you,
*"Consider him"*—Christ Jesus. You are afraid of God
because He hates sin. Your fears are based on truth.
God hates sin infinitely. If there were only one grain
of sin in the whole universe, He would burn it to
ashes to get rid of that grain of sin, for it is such a
detestable thing in His sight. But now consider
Christ Jesus, for sin was laid on Him.

If you will come now and put your trust in Jesus, you can be sure that your sin was laid on Christ
and the wrath of God concerning sin was expended
upon Him. The vials of Jehovah's indignation were
poured upon the devoted head of the Great Shepherd
of the sheep. God hates sin, but He will not hate you,
for you have no sin if you believe in Jesus, since your
sin is transferred to your surety and laid upon
Christ. You are clean.

Ah, but you say, "He is such a holy God, how
can I approach Him?" Well, I will tell you the most
blessed secret outside of heaven. It is this: you can,
by faith, put on the perfect righteousness of the Lord
Jesus, and when you have it on, you will be as holy
in the sight of God as Christ is holy. He has righteousness to spare, and He gives it to us, for He *"is
made unto us wisdom, and righteousness, and sanc-
tification, and redemption"* (1 Cor. 1:30).

When a soul puts on the righteousness of Christ by faith, even the all-seeing eye of God cannot see a flaw in that righteousness. Adam in the Garden had a perfect righteousness, but then it was only a human one. You and I, when we believe in Jesus, have a perfect righteousness that is divine—the righteousness of the Eternal Son of God Himself—and so we can come to God as if we had been perfectly innocent and can stand on terms of full familiarity with the Holy Trinity.

"Ah," says one, "there is good encouragement in all this, but I still have some dread remaining, for God is infinitely great." It is true, it is true, but I want you to *"consider him."* Remember, the God you are dealing with is not God as He appeared on Mount Sinai or, rather, as He was obscurely heard amid the dense darkness of the trembling mountain. But you are relating to God in Christ Jesus, and therefore, *"consider him."*

Now think for a minute. Jesus is our strong God, it is true. Do you not see Him walking on the water? But why does He pause in the midst of His wondrous passage over the waves? It is to stretch out His hand and save Peter from sinking, because he had cried, "Lord, save me, or I will perish." The strength of God will do the same for you as you are sinking and ready to perish. The omnipotent God will put out His hand and snatch you from the waves of fire and deliver your soul from destruction.

Consider Christ Jesus for a moment as our strong God and how He uses His strength. He walks down the streets where the sick lie in their beds, and does He trample on them and crush out the last spark of life from those poor wretches? No, but He touches this one, and an eye is opened. He puts His finger on another, and an ear is unstopped. He lays His hand on the dead, and they arise. Oh, yes, and He will do this to you.

Be thankful for a mighty God, for in Christ Jesus the omnipotence of God will only come to heal your troubles. See this omnipotent One take the loaves and the fishes in His hands and break them. As He breaks them, they multiply until all those thousands are fed out of one basket full of barley loaves and small fishes. He will feed your soul to the full with heavenly bread. His greatness will reveal itself in supplying your great needs and blessing you greatly. You will see it happen, if you will consider Jesus.

> Till God in human flesh I see
> My thoughts no comfort find;
> The holy, just, and sacred three,
> Are terrors to my mind.
>
> But if Immanuel's face appears,
> My hope, my joy begins,
> His name forbids my slavish fears,
> His grace forgives my sins.

## CONSIDER JESUS IN THE MIDST OF UNBELIEF

It may be that some soul is saying, "You have not touched my difficulty yet. I am troubled about sin, and I am troubled about God. But still, my greatest anxiety is this: I know that if I could believe, my sins would be pardoned, but I am perplexed with unbelief and greatly distressed because of the hardness of my heart, which will not let me repent." Come, then, soul, and *"consider him."*

## "Consider Him"

First, you say, "I have little or no faith." Then, *"consider him."* Did Jesus ever stipulate that people had to have great faith before He healed them? What trembling faith He accepted when He was on earth! The poor leper said, *"Lord, if thou wilt, thou canst make me clean"* (Matt. 8:2), and I know you can get as far as he did. And Jesus Christ said, *"I will; be thou clean"* (v. 3). A poor woman came into the crowd and was afraid to face the Master, but she crept behind Him and touched the hem of His garment and stole a cure, for she said, *"If I may touch but his clothes, I shall be whole"* (Mark 5:28). Jesus did not rebuke her, but He said, *"Thy faith hath made thee whole; go in peace"* (v. 34). So Jesus Christ loves even small faith. Therefore, I will talk to you as if you were characters in Bunyan's *The Pilgrim's Progress*: Much-afraid and Despondency, *"consider him"* and His gentleness towards the timid and trembling, and let your fears be gone.

But you say, "Ah, I am afraid, I have no faith at all." Then, beloved, *"consider him,"* and among other matters consider well how He deserves your faith. Tell me, what did Jesus ever do that you should doubt Him? He says He will save you if you will trust Him. Point to one promise He has broken. I challenge you; yes, I challenge all the world to point to one word that ever fell from His lips and was not fulfilled. That dear and precious Savior is truth itself. I feel I can trust Him, and whenever I do not trust Him, it is because I have not considered Him. The sight of Him makes me feel that I would rush into His arms. What, not trust Him who bears the earth's huge pillars up (Ps. 75:3)? I must trust Him!

Son of God and Son of Man, I see both Your strength and Your tenderness, and I must rely upon You. I pray that the man who feels that he cannot believe will consider Christ Jesus.

Think of Him in the garden; think of Him on the cross. Will His death not suffice? Think of Him as rising from the dead and pleading before the eternal throne.

> Venture on Him, venture wholly,
> Let no other trust intrude,
>    Sure this Savior
>    Can do helpless sinners good.

Well, then, suppose that after all you still say, "But I find that unbelief is still my trouble." Then I ask you to recollect that He was exalted on high on purpose so that He might bestow the gift of faith and repentance. Even while He was here on earth, His disciples prayed, Lord, *"Increase our faith"* (Luke 17:5), and you may without doubt pray to Him to give you faith. And you who mourn a hard heart, you may say, "Lord, You are exalted on high to give repentance to Israel (Acts 5:31); give repentance to me," for Jesus can touch your heart and make it tender in a moment. Only let that nail-pierced hand be laid upon your cold, petrified heart, and it will become warm and infused with heavenly life.

If you look to yourself to find repentance, you will look long enough, but if you will look to Him, is it not written, *"They shall look upon* [Him] *whom they have pierced, and they shall mourn for him, as one mourneth for...his firstborn"* (Zech. 12:10)? A sight of Christ produces repentance in the heart. Jesus looked on Peter; Peter's eyes were dry until then. But Peter saw that look, and it melted Peter's heart. Right through his nature it pierced like some mighty gleam of a tenfold sun. In a moment it pierced the iceberg of his nature and dissolved his soul. One look at Jesus will melt a heart of stone. *"Consider him,"* then.

Come to the point. You cannot believe or repent, but He can give you both belief and repentance. If you try to urge yourself to these, you will often make a mistake and make yourself more unbelieving and more unrepentant than before. But if you go to Christ for every grace that brings you near to Him and ask for them *"without money"* (Isa. 55:1), He will give you everything. He will freely bestow them upon you. If you let Him be Savior from top to bottom, from beginning to end; if you will just go to Him as helpless, lost, and ruined, and entrust yourself entirely to Him, you will find that He will not and cannot fail you in your time of need. Thus, you see, considering Him gets rid of those troubles. May the Spirit of God prove it to be so!

## CONSIDER JESUS DESPITE FAILINGS

Perhaps your own insignificance causes you to doubt. You complain and say, "I cannot think Christ would save me. I am nobody; I am inferior, poor, obscure." Dear friend, consider Jesus. Did He ever grovel at the great ones' feet? Did He preach in the royal chapel and there utter soft nothings, fit for the ears of kings and queens? You know He did not. He wore the clothing of the peasantry and called fishermen to be His apostles, thus pouring contempt on princes, for *"not many wise men after the flesh, not many mighty...are called"* (1 Cor. 1:26). He has chosen the low things of this world, and God has chosen such things to bring to nothing the things that are great.

"Ah," says one, "but I mean I have no gift or knowledge." Then *"consider him,"* and let me bring Him before your eyes. I see Him standing with uplifted hands, exclaiming,

> *I thank thee, O Father...because thou hast hid these things from the wise and prudent, and hast revealed them unto babes. Even so, Father: for so it seemed good in thy sight.*
> *(Matt. 11:25–26)*

Does that not settle that question once and for all? I am sure it ought to do so.

"Ah," says one, "but I am so unworthy." Yes, and will you tell me where Christ used to seek out the worthy ones? Did He not go and touch the eyes of blind beggars who were nothing but beggars and had no recommendation but poverty? Did He not bless those who had no claim by way of righteousness? Does mercy ever ask for merit? Does it not, on the contrary, seek those in misery? If an angel of mercy hovered over you, poising himself in midair, I would know that he did not come with mercy to one who is good and has no sin. Why should he come to insult you? But if you are a brokenhearted sinner, I know that the angel has a gracious word for you from the heart of Him who delights in mercy.

Do not say that you are a nobody and are therefore forgotten. Christ Jesus loves nobodies; He delights to pick up those whom society throws away.

The very offscourings and refuse are His choice. Solomon built his temple of cedar, but our Lord builds His temple with the most inferior woods in the forest. Any jeweler can make a precious thing out of gold, but Jesus makes diamonds out of dross and crowns out of clay.

"Ah," says one, "but I feel my powerlessness for everything that is good. I am sure that if I am to be saved, I cannot help in the process." Poor soul, it is strange that ever we should think we could help the Lord to save us. Could you have helped in creation? If you had been there when God was making the world, would you have offered to help Him? When He said, *"Let there be light"* (Gen. 1:3), would you have rushed forward with a match and said, "Permit me to add my little spark?" It is insulting to think of such a thing. But salvation is a greater work than creation. Stand back, you impertinent flesh and blood! You can only hinder the great work. God does not need your help. Humble yourself, and He will glorify Himself in your salvation.

"Still," says one, "I feel so feeble in everything I try to do. I tried to pray, but I could not." What did you do? "I was anxious because I could not pray." Well, you prayed much better than if you had thought you had prayed, for he who groans because he cannot pray has prayed the best prayer in the world. The poor publican did not say much, but when he struck his breast, even if he had not added the recorded words, he prayed. The act of striking his breast meant the true prayer of his soul: *"God be merciful to me a sinner"* (Luke 18:13).

"Ah," says one, "I have been trying to overcome sin lately, and I have been beaten." You will overcome by the blood of the Lamb, but all your own warring against sin will certainly end in defeat. Let the sword of the Lord and of Gideon be unsheathed, and the Midianites will soon be conquered. (See Judges 7.) But unless it is the sword of the Lord, there will be no defeat of your foes. *"Consider him,"* and have hope.

"Oh, but if I have any love for Christ, it is so little. If I have any faith, it is almost unbelief. If I have any life, it is but a flicker. How can I be saved?" Now, soul, once and for all be done with all this talk. Your salvation is in Christ and not in you. Do not say, "I have little strength." Confess that you have none at all, and then you are near the truth. Do not say, "I have little life." Confess that you are dead by nature, and you have hit the mark. Do not say, "I have little virtue." Say, "Since I am all unholy and unclean, I am nothing else but sin."

When you reach the bottom, you cannot fall lower, and that is the place where you ought to be. Jesus will never meet you until you come to the lowest point. Your extremity is His opportunity. When you are a beggar and do not even have a penny, then all Christ's richest treasures will be yours. But if you have a little to add to help the Savior, just so that you may have a side-glance at the glory of God, He will have nothing to do with you. He wants you, but He does not want anything that is yours. He wants your emptiness in order to fill it, but He wants nothing of your own to increase His fullness.

## CONSIDER JESUS DESPITE TEMPTATION

Perhaps there are some who say, "My case is different, for I am the subject of very fierce satanic temptations. Lately, I have been forced to endure such blasphemous thoughts and horrible suggestions that I can scarcely conceive any other human being has ever been subjected to them." Now, at once, *"consider him."*

> *For we have not an high priest which cannot be touched with the feeling of our infirmities; but was in all points tempted like as we are, yet without sin.* *(Heb. 4:15)*

I want you to remember this, and therefore to *"consider him."* Now, I know that if a preacher of the Gospel has had no temptations, nobody ever goes to him with questions of conscience. But if a man of God has been led through great adversity and soul trouble, all the distressed and afflicted people in the neighborhood are sure to fly to him because he can sympathize with them. Now, our dear Redeemer can sympathize with you who are tempted by the Devil, for He was in the wilderness for forty days and tempted by Satan, too. Go to Him. "But I am afraid of the temptations I will have in years to come." Are you? Then, *"consider him,"* for *"he is able also to save them to the uttermost that come unto God by him, seeing he ever liveth to make intercession for them"* (Heb. 7:25).

What a choice word He had for Peter, *"Satan hath desired to have you, that he may sift you as wheat: but I have prayed for thee, that thy faith fail not"* (Luke 22:31–32). Oh, poor soul, consider Jesus, and remember that if all the devils in hell were to tempt you, and you had only Jesus Christ present with you, you would no more need to be afraid than if the dogs in the streets were to bark at your heels when all their teeth had been pulled. Jesus has broken the Devil's teeth by the power of His intercession. He has power to howl at us, but he cannot bite us. With a malicious joy, he troubles those whom he cannot devour, but the Lord has struck our enemy on the cheekbone. By one tremendous blow of His pierced hand, He has broken the teeth of the Oppressor.

I hear yet another cry. "Come here," says one, "I have something to whisper in your ear that I can hardly tell. My trouble is about my inward corruption. Oh, if ever there is an unclean heart in all the world, I have it. It is like some foul pond that bubbles up with putrid gas. My inmost nature is filled with all manner of filthiness and iniquity, like a mud volcano that pours forth a horrid stream. Oh, sir, my heart is abominable; a cage of unclean birds is nothing compared to it; it is a den of devils." Well, well, *"consider him."*

You remember how He came into the temple and there were the buyers and sellers with their bulls and sheep and doves. I have often marveled at the ease with which He drove them out. He did not even have a rope with Him, only a few small cords, but He began immediately to strike out at those around Him. And, oh, how they ran. Those money-grubbers, who would not have lost a shekel for their lives, saw their gold and silver spilled on the ground while the bulls and the sheep fled from the holy place and the doves fluttered out into the air. Let Christ come into your heart, and He will soon drive out the buyers and sellers, and the old Dragon himself.

Remember, too, that Jesus is the Creator. He made the heavens and the earth—can He not create you anew? Is it not said, *"He that sat upon the throne said, Behold, I make all things new"* (Rev. 21:5)? Consider His omnipotent power. Having given you a new heart, can He not make you completely holy? Oh, do not think so continually of your sin and sinfulness and propensity for transgression, but think of Christ, almighty to save. Whether you sink or swim, cast yourself upon Him. Lost or saved, come and cling to His cross, and I guarantee you that you will not perish; eternal life will be the portion of everyone who rests in Him.

## CONSIDER JESUS DESPITE FEAR

Still, somebody says, "I am troubled about the three last things. I am afraid of death, judgment, hell." Afraid of death? Well, but if you will only trust the Son of God who died for sinners, you never need to be afraid to die. When your little child has run about and wearied herself and wants to sleep—is she afraid to fall asleep in her mother's arms with her head on her mother's breast? And you, dear child of God, when you are wearied with your work, you will go and lay your head on Jesus' chest and fall asleep, and it will be just as easy and just as sweet as for your little ones to sleep in your arms.

"But I am afraid of judgment," says one. Judgment? Your judgment is past already. Your sins were judged in Christ and punished in Christ, if you believe in Him. The sins of all believers were brought before the court of judgment and condemned and destroyed in Christ. Let us go back to that famous passage by Paul for a minute. He pictured God's chosen people standing before the throne, and he cried, *"Who shall lay any thing to the charge of God's elect?"* (Rom. 8:33). Who is afraid of judgment when nobody can lay anything to his charge? And then Paul went on to say, *"Who is he that condemneth?"* (v. 34). No one can condemn but the Judge, and who is He? It is Christ who died, and can He who died for us condemn us? Impossible. He cannot contradict Himself. So you do not need to be afraid of judgment.

"But I am afraid of hell," says one. Ah, and there is good reason to fear it. Fear him who can destroy both body and soul in hell (Matt. 10:28); I say to you, fear him. But you do not need to fear hell if you trust in Jesus, for Christ has suffered the punishment of your sin, and as far as you are concerned, hell is nothing to worry about. There are no flames of wrath for you; they have consumed themselves on the Savior. When the Jew laid his sin offering on the altar and the fire consumed it, the sinful Jew stood there and said, "That sacrifice stands for me." When it was all burned, he said, "My sins are burned. And when they took the ashes into an unclean place and utterly consumed them, my sin was put away. They have put it outside the camp; it has been consumed forever."

So when we *"consider him,"* even our dear Lord Jesus on the cross, we see Him there, a complete sacrifice, the fire of God roasting and burning Him up, consuming Him from the inside out until He is utterly consumed as a sacrifice. There our sin was annihilated. Every believer may know that there his sin ceased to be, for it is written, "He has finished the transgression. He has made an end of sin, and has brought in an everlasting righteousness." (See Daniel 9:24.)

As I conclude my discussion of this subject, it is with this earnest prayer: may every seeking sinner believe in Jesus at once. Oh, weary one, why do you not rest upon Him? Wanderer, you will never find rest until you come to Jesus! Seeker, your seeking is in vain if you will not have my Lord! Trembler, your tremblings themselves are to be trembled at, if they keep you from the Cross! There is the Savior, to be received without money and without price. He has been proclaimed to you. Believe Him, that is, trust Him and live forever! May the Lord bless you now and compel you by His mercy to do so, for Jesus' sake. Amen.